The Generous Corporation

NEIL J. MITCHELL

The Generous Corporation

A Political Analysis of Economic Power

YALE UNIVERSITY PRESS

NEW HAVEN AND LONDON

Published with assistance from the Samuel W. Meek
Publication Fund.

Designed by Jo Aerne and set in Melior type with
Optima for display by Brevis Press, Bethany, Con-
necticut. Printed in the United States of America by
BookCrafters, Inc., Chelsea, Michigan.

Library of Congress Cataloging-in-Publication Data
Mitchell, Neil J.
    The generous corporation : a political analysis of
economic power
    Neil J. Mitchell.
    p. cm.
    Includes index.
    ISBN 0–300–04413–5 (alk. paper)
    1. Industry—Social aspects—United
States. 2. Corporations—Political aspects—United
States. 3. Industrial management—United
States. I. Title.
HD60.5.U5M59 1989   88–14417
302.3′5—dc19   CIP

The paper in this book meets the guidelines for per-
manence and durability of the Committee on Production Guidelines for Book Longevity of the
Council on Library Resources.

10 9 8 7 6 5 4 3 2 1

For my parents
James and Agnes Mitchell

We feel ourselves caught in the whirl of new forces, and flung forward every day a step farther into a future dim with the portents of struggle between Titans reared on steam, electricity, and credit. It is an unfortunate moment for the break-down of the science that claimed to be able to reconcile self-interest with the harmony of interests.

Henry D. Lloyd

Contents

Acknowledgments

This work began as a dissertation at Indiana University, where I received help from Byrum Carter, Alfred Diamant, Norman Furniss, and Timothy Tilton of the Department of Political Science, and David Martin of the Department of Business Economics. Norman Furniss first drew my attention to the topic of corporate social responsibility and provided invaluable advice and encouragement throughout the project. Charles Anderson of the University of Wisconsin–Madison was kind enough to read and comment on the entire work. I would also like to thank Gerald Wright and Russell Hanson of Indiana University and Lee Preston of the University of Maryland for their comments on chapter 3, and Mack Shelley of Iowa State University for his comments on chapter 9. Marian Neal Ash and Harry Haskell of Yale University Press and the outside reviewer all made helpful suggestions. I am grateful to Susan Mitchell for her support and editorial help, and to James F. Mitchell for monitoring the British business press.

I was fortunate to do my graduate work in the stimulating environment of the Political Science Department at Indiana University and to discuss parts of this work with a number of my fellow students—in particular, Christi Barbour, Philippe LePrestre, and David Robertson. Finally, I would like to thank the Department of Political Science at Iowa State University for providing research support for this project. Versions of chapters 3 and 5 appeared in Lee Preston, ed., *Research in Corporate Social Performance and Policy*, vol. 5 (Greenwich, Conn.: JAI Press, 1983) and in the *Western Political Quarterly* 38 (June 1986), respectively.

The Generous Corporation

one

The Spirit of American Capitalism

"To suggest social action for the public good to the City of London," John Maynard Keynes commented in 1926, "is like discussing the *Origin of Species* with a bishop sixty years ago."[1] President Reagan, not one of the Keynesian persuasion, is more optimistic about contemporary American businessmen. He expects an attentive audience for his suggestions about the social role of the private sector. He believes businessmen capable of unselfish as well as selfish actions that contribute to social well-being. His effort to diminish public responsibility for the people's economic and social security was predicated on an anticipation that businessmen would become increasingly responsive to society's problems. "Together, we have begun to mobilize the private sector—not to duplicate wasteful and discredited Government programs but to . . . help solve many of America's social problems," the President said in his 1982 State of the Union message.

American businessmen appear willing to accept the challenge. The chief executive of Coca Cola says, "Today we are beginning to get the opportunity we have wanted for so long to prove that when private enterprise is relatively free, it can be the primary agent of response to human need."[2] The chief executive of Control Data comments, "For too long business has been preoccupied doing things that are most profitable and leaving the solutions to most of

---

1. "The End of Laissez-Faire," *The Collected Writings of John Maynard Keynes*, vol. 9 (London: Macmillan, 1972), p. 287.
2. Quoted in Bailey Morris, "Welfare Challenge to US Business," *The Times*, July 30, 1982, p. 15.

the major problems to government."[3] According to the chairman of Dupont, it is not enough for a corporation simply to make products; "the larger it is, the more it is expected to assume various obligations that once were met by individuals or communities, or were not met at all."[4] Even John De Lorean, better known for making sports cars in Northern Ireland and narcotics-related court appearances in California, chastises current General Motors executives for being indifferent to the corporation's "many publics" and bemoans a lack of "industrial statesmanship."[5] Monsanto, as a matter of policy, devotes 2 percent of its profits to social projects; in 1980 the firm donated $6.4 million to community causes.[6] IBM is the biggest giver among American corporations, having contributed more than $100 million in 1984.

Money is not the only form of corporate philanthropy. Businesses also make gifts of products, equipment, and expertise. Nabisco donates food to the needy. Exxon, aware of the decline in public support for legal aid, makes its expertise available in this area. Total corporate contributions in 1987 (the latest year for which figures are available) were estimated at $4.5 billion.[7] Although this figure does not come close to matching recent government cuts in social spending—and, in any case, the objectives of governmental and corporate spending differ—it represents a substantial commitment that affects corporate administrative structures, as well as the cost of doing business. Many firms appoint management committees, staffed by senior officials, to oversee their social policies. Despite the current emphasis social responsibility is neither an ephemeral outcome of presidential exhortation nor a recent development; it is an institutionalized and continuing function of the modern large corporation.

3. *Fortune*, November 19, 1979, p. 42.

4. Peter Behr, "Business Confronts Social Issues," *The Washington Post*, January 21, 1982, p. G4.

5. J. Patrick Wright, *On a Clear Day You Can See General Motors* (New York: Avon, 1979), pp. 270–75.

6. Arnold Kransdorff, "Reacting to the Social Pulse," *The Financial Times*, July 27, 1981, p. 9.

7. *The Financial Times*, May 4, 1988, p. 22.

Many people view corporate philanthropy as a postwar phenomenon, a responsibility hurriedly assumed to quell the discontent of the 1960s, to keep the smoke of the burning ghetto away from the office window, or perhaps to make amends for creating such lethal products as napalm. Actually, social responsibility is characteristic of the modern corporation, although its substance and salience change over time. It was first visibly demonstrated in the springtime of corporate America, the 1920s, a decade before the state had a social responsibility to abdicate. Although isolated initiatives were undertaken in the late nineteenth century, it was not until the second and particularly the third decades of the twentieth century that corporate social policy became widespread. Businessmen established pension plans, employee stock ownership and life insurance schemes, unemployment funds, limitations on working hours, and high wages. They built houses, churches, schools, and libraries, provided medical and legal services, and gave to charity. The quality of these philanthropic endeavors varied. But what is remarkable about corporate social policy, as Dr. Johnson once said about dogs walking on their hind legs, is not that it is not done well but that it is done at all.

Although social responsibility is sometimes described as consistent with maximizing profits in the long run, Carl Kaysen writes that

the uncertainty attached to some benefits (say those of being a high-wage employer), the difficulty of translating into cash terms others (such as maintaining good community relations), the remoteness in time of still others (such as supporting liberal arts education) indicate that profit maximization must be given a very elastic interpretation indeed to cover all these activities. While all who use words may avail themselves of Humpty-Dumpty's privilege, there appears to be some merit in recognizing a difference between profit maximization as traditionally conceived, which concerns itself with inflows of cash to the firm which can be estimated with some degree of definiteness, and the kind of policies I have been describing.[8]

8. "The Social Significance of the Modern Corporation," *American Economic Review* 47 (May 1957), p. 313.

Corporate social policies whose benefits are not restricted to those who bear the costs, such as support for liberal arts education, make it more difficult to explain these activities solely in terms of maximizing profits. Critics of corporate social responsibility—and there are some—argue that it is fundamentally opposed to the profit motive and, as a consequence, produces generally detrimental results. In the eyes of Theodore Levitt, Milton Friedman, Irving Kristol, or Friedrich Hayek, corporate social responsibility is unbusinesslike and thus not only threatens the survival of individual corporations but also undermines the general vitality of capitalism.[9]

What has happened to the business firm, that cradle of utility maximization, economic man's natural habitat? What makes businessmen construct plans for the welfare of their employees and the community? What accounts for corporate social responsibility, or, as it has been defined, "voluntary restraint of profit maximization"?[10] Even if it were possible to directly reconcile social responsibility with the profit motive, one would still have to ask why businessmen visibly pursue goodwill rather than relying, as they have traditionally, on the operation of an "invisible hand" to transform selfish motives into public benefits. Why has the robber baron's ostentatious delight in profit been replaced by the industrial statesman's equally ostentatious concern for social responsibility? This book addresses these questions from a variety of perspectives. The analysis is set, for the most part, in the first three decades of the twentieth century, a decisive historical moment when the American corporation achieved its modern form and businessmen's motivations and practices began to change. By looking at the origins of corporate social policy, it is possible to isolate significant related changes that influenced corporate policy makers.

9. Levitt, "The Dangers of Social Responsibility," *Harvard Business Review* 36 (September–October 1958); Friedman, *Capitalism and Freedom* (Chicago: University of Chicago Press, 1962); Kristol, *Two Cheers for Capitalism* (New York: Basic Books, 1978); Hayek, *Studies in Philosophy, Politics and Economics* (Chicago: University of Chicago Press, 1967).

10. Kenneth R. Andrews, "Can The Best Corporations Be Made Moral?" *Harvard Business Review* 51 (May–June 1973), p. 57.

The effort to fit corporate social responsibility into long-run profit maximization does not exhaust attempts to find an explanation in terms of economic categories. One plausible explanation of corporate social policy, popular among economists, is to relate it to the organization of property rights in the modern corporation. At least since Adolf Berle and Gardiner Means wrote *The Modern Corporation and Private Property* in 1932, economists have called attention to the progressive separation of ownership from control. With ownership dispersed and salaried managers running the corporation, concerns other than profit may begin to guide corporate activity. Berle and Means were convinced that managers, increasingly conscious of claims from groups other than stockholders, would become less profit-oriented. Adding to the plausibility of this explanation is that the separation of ownership from control, a definitive characteristic of the modern corporation in mainstream social science, was already reported to be well advanced when corporate social policy first developed on a wide scale.

Alternatively, corporate social responsibility has been viewed as a sop to labor, rather than as the result of an undesigned organizational change within the corporation or a sign of a new and more humane industrial order. Employers, in this view, have switched tactics by substituting inducement for repression. The social policies of the 1920s are accounted for by the necessity of combating unionization and purchasing industrial peace to protect corporate profits.

On examination, each of these explanations turns out to be at best inadequate. In this book, the modern corporation is treated as a political institution and corporate social responsibility is analyzed in terms of political concepts. The study of politics constituted by what states do is a conventional, not a logical, restriction of focus. Other institutions in society besides the state possess power, and no substantive definition of public policy can exclude nonstate activity. As businesses like the Corrections Corporation of America begin to build, buy, and run prisons, even what were once thought of, in the liberal tradition at least, as "core" state functions—such as maintaining law and order—are now performed by the private sector. There is no definition of the policy process, be-

yond a formalism, that excludes nonstate institutions. State policy
may be arrived at in either a democratic or a dictatorial way. If
pluralist theory is right, the source of policy made by states is in
any case the successful exertion of pressure by an association of
individuals, perhaps a private corporation. However, institutions
differ in the amount of power they possess, assessed in terms of
the size of the community affected. By this measure the large corporation has become the most important new institution in the
contemporary political order; production, consumption, even significant aspects of state action fall within its orbit.

Other observers have treated the corporation as a political institution. Democratic theorists have argued that it should be considered an appropriate arena for political activity because its smaller
size makes participatory democracy possible in the era of the na-
tion-state. And Robert Dahl's principle of affected interest allows
him to make a case for some form of worker self-management.[11] The
idea of the corporation as a political system runs throughout Dahl's
published work. While approaching the topic with a different problem in mind than that of Dahl and the democratic theorists, I suggest that the corporation is a legitimate subject for political analysis.
Although taking a different route, by investigating the connections
between the political concepts of power, legitimacy, ideology, and
policy within the context of the corporation, we arrive in the end
at issues of concern to students of democratic theory.

If it is accepted that corporations have power, then they, like the
state, face the problem of legitimizing their power. That power requires legitimacy is one of the classical axioms of politics. Hume
begins his essay "Of the First Principles of Government" with these
words:

> Nothing appears more surprising to those who consider
> human affairs with a philosophical eye than the easiness
> with which the many are governed by the few, and the
> implicit submission with which men resign their own
> sentiments and passions to those of their rulers. When we
> inquire by what means this wonder is effected, we shall

11. *After the Revolution* (New Haven: Yale University Press, 1970).

find that, as force is always on the side of the governed,
the governors have nothing to support them but opinion.
It is, therefore, on opinion only that government is
founded, and this maxim extends to the most despotic
and most military governments as well as to the most free
and most popular. The soldan of Egypt or the emperor of
Rome might drive his harmless subjects like brute beasts
against their sentiments and inclination. But he must, at
least, have led his mamalukes [sic] or praetorian bands,
like men, by their opinion.[12]

Opinion is shaped, and legitimacy is provided, by ideology. Corporate social policies originated as an expression of a new ideology
of business power. They represented an attempt to legitimize that
power in the eyes of government and other groups.

The legitimacy problems encountered by corporations signified
that the economy was outgrowing the old means of justification. At
the turn of the century the classical economic equation of private
interest with public good was becoming increasingly strained. Consumption, even to some economists, was now more conspicuous
than the operation of the "invisible hand." Businessmen in the rapidly expanding corporate sector could not easily rely on an ideology
theoretically grounded in perfect competition to interpret their own
experience—and to answer a growing number of critics. The new
business ideology that emerged in the early twentieth century expanded business priorities to include social responsibility and
sought publicly to establish the notion of a "good" corporation.

Of course, the significance placed here on the relationship between ideas and business conduct, and on the need capitalists feel
to justify their activities, is at least as old as Max Weber's work on
the historical development of capitalism. In his foreword to Weber's
Protestant Ethic and the Spirit of Capitalism, R. H. Tawney described
Calvinism as "the tonic that braced the bourgeoisie for the conflict"

12. David Hume, "Of the First Principles of Government," in Henry D.
Aiken, ed., *Hume's Moral and Political Philosophy* (New York: Hafner Press,
1948), p. 307.

with the aristocracy.[13] The present study focuses on the ideology that has served as the tonic for American corporate management in their struggles with working-class organizations or disaffected members of the middle class— from the Progressives to the environmentalists. It examines the causes, contents, and consequences of business ideology in attempting to explain corporate social responsibility.

Finally, it is worth saying a word about why a political scientist should be interested in this topic. Social life does not always comply with the intellectual divisions represented by the disciplines of social science. Political scientists' enthusiasm for seeing their field of study colonized by other social scientists, particularly economists, is well known.[14] Viewing corporations as political institutions reverses this process by applying political analysis to a preeminently economic institution. In crossing between disciplines, a deeper multidimensional appreciation of a problem becomes possible. The effort to explain corporate social policy raises a variety of issues that are significant for contemporary social and political theory. These include the separation of ownership from control within the corporation, the relationship of ideology to policy, and the nature of ideological change. Furthermore, the activities of business and the private sector influence what the public sector does. It is possible, for example, that corporate social policies and the ideology behind them retarded the development of public-sector social policies. The American government was much slower to get involved in this area than were the governments of other industrial countries. This "American exceptionalism" is often attributed to the weakness of the American working class, but the power of business should also be considered. Finally, and more generally, the attitudes and actions of corporate decision makers are important in themselves. Corporate budgets are often compared to those of nation-states, though even this does not properly illustrate the unparalleled position of business in American life. In England or

13. *The Protestant Ethic and the Spirit of Capitalism* (London: Allen and Unwin, 1930), p. 2.

14. See Albert O. Hirschman, *Exit, Voice and Loyalty* (Cambridge, Mass.: Harvard University Press, 1970).

France the bright and ambitious aim for the civil service; in America they go to business school. A tourist's itinerary in America includes such monuments to corporate success as the Sears Tower in Chicago, not castles, cathedrals, and ancient ruins. As Carl Jung put it in 1912, "The Libido of American man is focused almost entirely on his business."[15]

15. William McGuire and R. F. C. Hulls, eds., *C. G. Jung Speaking: Interviews and Encounters* (London: Picador, 1980), p. 39.

two

Brave New Business:
Corporate Social Policies in the 1920s

The Fuggers, the great medieval capitalists, recognized social responsibilities. Apart from patronizing the arts, at Augsburg they
built "out of piety and as an example of especial generosity" the
Fuggerei, a village for those of their fellow-citizens who were "up-
right but impoverished."[1] Some three centuries later Robert Owen
attracted considerable attention with his attempt to construct a
more kindly industrial world in the Scottish village of New Lanark;
even the Czar of Russia paid him a visit. Across the Atlantic in
Lowell, Massachusetts, mill owners established a health care program and built dormitories, supervised by matrons, to provide for
the moral well-being of their young female workers.[2]

Capitalist philanthropy is probably as old as capitalism itself.
Richard Sennett, in his article "Our Hearts Belong to Daddy," argues
that paternalism is the common thread that runs from New Lanark
to the social policies of IBM, via Lowell and Pullman, Illinois. Employers apparently have always been eager to fulfill the universal
human need for a father. A distinction, however, can be made between corporate social policy in the 1920s and the philanthropy
represented by isolated instances of paternalism in the nineteenth
century and before. Quirks of individual character and social circumstances can account for the curiosities of earlier centuries, but

1. Miriam Beard, *A History of the Business Man* (New York: Macmillan,
1938), pp. 241–42.
2. Richard Sennett, "Our Hearts Belong to Daddy," *New York Review of
Books*, May 1, 1980, p. 32.

not for the spread of corporate social policy in the 1920s. In 1929 the Committee on Recent Economic Changes of the President's Conference on Unemployment concluded: "It is generally recognized that there has been a voluntary assumption by employers of heavy social charges in the establishment of benefits of various kinds."[3] The popularity of corporate social policy among businessmen in the 1920s indicates that something had indeed changed. A general explanation in terms of paternalism would have to show why "Daddy" became so important and so popular at this time; an analysis of structural and ideological change in the American economy is likely to be more fruitful.

Corporate social policies, sometimes referred to as "welfare capitalism" or "industrial betterment," included a large number of activities, directed both internally at employees and externally at the community. Among them were pensions and life insurance (before either became an object for collective bargaining or an anticipated fringe benefit), high wages, employee stock ownership (when stock was given or sold to employees without financial advantage to the company), various schemes for unemployment prevention and insurance, medical services, and gifts to charity. The internally directed policies might appear to fit more easily into an economic explanation of corporate social policy, but they represented a cost to the firm, voluntarily incurred, in return for which the benefits were very difficult to calculate. And if businessmen did expect tangible returns, why should they now want to induce good behavior from employees rather than order it? In fact, corporations found these policies useful in persuading critics that they were exercising their power justly. The Bureau of Labor Statistics' "Welfare Work for Employees in Industrial Establishments in the United States" (1919) provides a good definition of corporate social policy: "anything for the comfort and improvement, intellectual or social, of the employees, over and above wages paid, which is not a necessity of the industry nor required by law." Similarly, the *Encyclopaedia of Social Science* (1931) defined welfare work as "the voluntary efforts of an employer to establish, within the existing industrial system, working and sometimes living and cultural conditions of his em-

---

3. *Recent Economic Changes* (New York: McGraw-Hill, 1929), p. 5.

ployees beyond what is required by law, the customs of the industry, and the conditions of the market."[4] While capturing the essentially voluntary nature of corporate social policy in the sense of an absence of market or legal constraints, these definitions need expanding to include the community as well as employees.

In 1914 the Ford Motor Company reduced its working day to eight hours, instituted three shifts instead of two, and introduced a five-dollar basic daily wage. Company policy stated that no one seeking a job should be turned down because of his physical condition, unless he had a contagious disease, and that no one should be discharged for physical disability. Allan Nevins, arguing that unions were ineffectual in Detroit at the time, denies that the firm's primary motivation was to reduce labor turnover. Instead, he attributes these policies to the humanity of the employer: "Not since New Lanark had a bolder effort been made to raise the standards of working class life than that now instituted by the Ford Company."[5] Robert Owen was an odd man, and so no doubt was Henry Ford. But while New Lanark was an isolated curiosity of early capitalism, Ford's labor policies were more or less in tune with the times.

In 1922 Standard Oil of New Jersey established a welfare program that included the following points:

- No discrimination by the company or its employees against any employee on account of membership . . . . [in a] union.
- Collective dealing as to all matters of mutual interest, made effective through the industrial representation plan.
- Paying at least the prevailing scale of wages.
- The eight-hour day.
- Payment of disability benefits in case of accidents incurred while at work.
- Health supervision by competent medical staff.
- Payment of sickness benefits after one year's service.

4. U.S. Bureau of Labor Statistics, "Welfare Work for Employees in Industrial Establishments in the United States," *Bulletin no. 250* (Washington, D.C.: U.S. Government Printing Office, 1919), p. 8; and *Encyclopaedia of Social Science* (New York: Macmillan, 1931), p. 395.

5. *Ford: The Times, The Man, The Company* (New York: Scribner's, 1954), vol. 1, p. 552.

- One week's annual vacation with pay . . . . extended to two weeks after five years' service.
- Partnership through employee stock ownership, the company adding to the amount invested by the employee.
- Assurance of an annuity at the age of sixty-five.
- Death benefits or insurance for dependents of employees with one year or more of service.[6]

Clarence Hicks, an influential propagandist for corporate social policies, helped formulate the Standard Oil program, having previously assisted with the International Harvester scheme. According to Hicks, International Harvester "was the first great corporation in America to assume responsibility for industrial accidents, far in advance of any state or federal legislation on workmen's compensation."[7] In his autobiography Hicks admits to failing to persuade Tolstoy, whom he visited on a trip to Russia, of the worth of this approach to the problems of modern industrial society—Tolstoy advised a return to the farm. Fortunately, American businessmen were more tractable than Russian novelists.

Corporate social policy had organizational as well as individual promoters. The National Civic Federation, formed in 1900, recognized at the outset the importance of social policies. Among its members were Andrew Carnegie, George Perkins (J. Pierpont Morgan's associate), Samuel Gompers, John Mitchell (president of the miners' union), and John R. Commons (Wisconsin economist). The NCF had a welfare department, which held conferences for employers and distributed literature to stimulate interest in welfare activity. By 1915 this organization claimed that it was entitled to much of the credit for changing "the thoughts and conduct of the great army of progressive employers who are today giving consideration to the conditions surrounding their employees in this country."[8]

Textbooks were published for interested employers. Lee Frankel

6. Clarence Hicks, *My Life in Industrial Relations* (New York: Harper and Bros., 1941), p. 57.

7. Ibid., p. 42.

8. Marguerite Green, *The National Civic Federation and the American Labor Movement, 1900–1925* (Washington, D.C.: Catholic University Press of America, 1956), p. 269.

and Alexander Fleisher, in *The Human Factor in Industry*, saw welfare policies as a matter of industrial efficiency and paternalism as the cardinal sin. They tell the cautionary tale of the Pullman Company, whose paternalistic policies were held responsible for one of the more famous strikes in American labor history in 1894.[9] George Pullman ran an industrial autocracy and treated workers as "his children." His paternalism, however, was spiced with a healthy desire for profit, and the strike may actually have been precipitated by a wage cut.

Table 2.1 shows the development of some corporate social policies during the first three decades of this century. While relatively few companies were involved in the first decade, the policies spread rapidly and became a common corporate activity in the 1920s. For example, the amount of life insurance that corporations provided for their employees rose from about $13 million in 1912 to about $10 billion in 1930. In 1930 it was estimated that approximately eight million employees were benefiting from this form of insurance. The average coverage was $1,200 per person. Apart from a temporary reduction in 1921, coinciding with an economic depression, life insurance grew steadily during this period, and the rate of growth of group life insurance was much greater than that of ordinary life insurance.[10] Group insurance was provided by an insurance company for employees on behalf of their employer. Industrial life insurance did not require individual medical examinations for eligibility. Instead, the factory itself was often inspected, with high-risk industries paying higher premiums. In a 1929 study by the National Industrial Conference Board of 618 companies operating insurance schemes, 439 had eligibility requirements of a length of service varying from two weeks to five years; most required between three and six months. Of these companies, 417 had schemes that covered their entire work force. The premium, based on the average age of the participants, was paid either entirely by

9. Lee K. Frankel and Alexander Fleisher, *The Human Factor in Industry* (New York: Macmillan, 1920), p. 269.

10. National Industrial Conference Board, *Industrial Group Insurance* (New York, 1929), p. 3; "Group Insurance," *Encyclopaedia of Social Science* (1931), p. 183.

Table 2.1   Corporate Social Policies, 1900–1930

Year	Life insurance[a]	Pension plans	Employee stock purchase plans	Employee representation plans	Charitable contributions[b]
1900	—	12	3	—	—
1905	—	36	14	—	—
1910	0.1	66	13	—	—
1915	—	167	30	—	—
1920	1.5	287	111	145	2.5
1925	4.0	359	162	432	9.0
1930	10.0	418	—	313	13.0

Sources: National Industrial Conference Board, *Industrial Group Insurance* (New York, 1929); *Encyclopaedia of Social Science* (New York: Macmillan, 1931); Murray Latimer, *Industrial Pension Systems* (New York: Industrial Counselors, 1932); National Industrial Conference Board, *Employee Stock Purchase Plans in the United States* (New York, 1928); National Industrial Conference Board, *Collective Bargaining Through Employee Representation* (New York, 1933); Pierce Williams and Frederick Croxton, *Corporate Contributions to Organized Community Welfare Services* (New York: National Bureau of Economic Research, 1930).
[a]Amount of life insurance held by insurance carriers in $billions. The figures for 1910 and 1930 are estimates.
[b]Corporate contributions to community chests in $millions

the employer or jointly by the employee and the employer. The tendency during the 1920s was to move from noncontributory to contributory plans—a shift that some have interpreted as an attempt to dispel any trace of paternalism.[11] Life insurance was gradually extended to include disability clauses, which provided for payment to workers who were permanently disabled on the job. These were apparently one of the most popular features of industrial insurance among employees.[12] Because no medical examinations were required, a sizeable proportion of employees—about 20 percent—got insurance for which they would not otherwise have been eligible. On the other hand, industrial life insurance was contingent on employment and did not offer the permanency of coverage provided

11. *Industrial Group Insurance*, pp. 20–22; "Group Insurance," p. 184.
12. "Group Insurance Experience of Various Establishments," *Monthly Labor Review* 24 (June 1927), p. 79.

by an individual policy.[13] Before group insurance, the only sources
of similar protection within the factory were mutual benefit associations. These were formed primarily on the initiative of employees, but employers made financial contributions and carried most
of the administrative costs.[14]

Few industrial pension plans were established before the turn of
the century, but from 1900 their popularity rapidly increased (see
table 2.1). The railroad companies and others associated with them
were the first to establish old-age pension schemes in the United
States. The American Express Company began a noncontributory
plan in 1875. The Baltimore and Ohio Railroad Company introduced a contributory plan in 1880, and the Pennsylvania Lines
established a pension scheme in 1900. By 1905, 35 percent of all
railroad employees were covered by pension schemes. The railroad's leading role in establishing industrial pension schemes is
connected to the fact that firms in this industry were the first to
achieve large size.[15] Public utilities were the next major industrial
group to introduce pension policies, followed by manufacturing
companies. By the mid-1920s most of the larger firms had pension
plans based on age and length of service. International Harvester
established a scheme in 1908 under which all employees, except
executives, were entitled to pensions at age seventy, provided they
had twenty or more years of service. The company paid the full
cost and apparently the pension was quite generous.[16] In 1930 the
average annual industrial pension benefit was $700. In manufac-
turing, oil companies paid the best pensions, with a $1,394 average
benefit. The overall average for manufacturing companies was $602.
Public utility companies generally paid higher pensions than manufacturing companies or railroads. Under noncontributory plans,
pensions were usually paid as they came due out of the firm's cur-

13. "Group Insurance," p. 185.

14. See National Industrial Conference Board, *The Present Status of Mutual
Benefit Associations* (New York, 1931).

15. Murray W. Latimer, *Industrial Pension Systems in the United States and
Canada* (New York: Industrial Relations Counsellors, 1932), vol. 1, pp. 20–35.

16. Robert Ozanne, *A Century of Labor-Management Relations at McCormick
and International Harvester* (Madison: University of Wisconsin Press, 1967),
pp. 83–84.

rent operating expenses. Many industrial pension plans ran into financial trouble because employers underestimated the rapidly growing costs. In 1928 only 35 percent of the 307 companies with noncontributory plans were accumulating funds for the payment of future benefits.[17]

From the worker's viewpoint, a common defect of many company pension plans, including Harvester's, was that they conferred no legal entitlement on employees. Many contained clauses that permitted employers to withhold or terminate plans at their discretion. Companies uncertain of their own continued financial security were reluctant to provide absolute guarantees for their employees. Yet some plans did exempt retired employees from the discretionary powers of employers.[18] There was a tendency during the 1920s toward removing discretionary features and requiring contributions from employees. In 1929 about 23 percent of all plans were contributory and an estimated 3.5 million employees—or 14 percent of the total—were covered by company plans.[19] In 1932, 140,000 workers received pensions worth $97 million. But the depression affected both the survival of the pension plans and the level of benefits. The period from 1929 to 1932 marked the highest rate of termination of plans, and 30 percent of eligible employees received reduced benefits.[20]

From the corporation's perspective, the economic benefits of pension plans were negligible. As early as 1920, a study by the Merchants' Association of New York found that these plans had minimal effect on labor turnover; Murray Latimer later corroborated this conclusion. Nor did pensions serve as an excuse to pay lower wages. On average, wages in companies with pension plans were 14 percent higher than the industry norms.[21] In general, corporate social policy makers paid higher wages than those who did not make social policy.[22] Although pensions represented an economic

17. Latimer, vol. 1, pp. 223—24; vol. 2, p. 615.
18. Ibid., vol. 2, p. 742.
19. Ibid., vol. 1, p. 48.
20. Ibid., vol. 2, p. 886.
21. Ibid., vol. 2, pp. 752 and 778.
22. National Industrial Conference Board, *Industrial Relations Programs in Small Plants* (New York, 1929), p. 42.

cost to the corporation, employers did not treat these policies in a businesslike fashion. Little effort was made to estimate future costs of pension plans, and almost none to evaluate what economic benefits, if any, these plans produced. Only two of the nearly four hundred companies in Latimer's survey reported any attempt to measure economic gains in terms of payroll relief. Aside from businessmen's humanitarian motives, Latimer attributes industrial pension plans primarily to pressure from public opinion.[23] That political as well as economic benefits now figured in employers' calculations illustrates the difference between the 1920s and the robber baron era.

In 1921 the magazine *Management Review* said of company plans to make stock available to employees that "no movement is destined to become a factor of greater significance in changing industrial conditions."[24] With the largest corporations leading the movement, approximately one million employees owned stock by 1927.[25] In 1926, 44 percent (19,135) of the stockholders of Standard Oil of New Jersey, 55 percent (12,000) of International Harvester's stockholders, and 63 percent (35,000) of Bethlehem Steel Company's stockholders were employees. However, the actual market values of employee stockholdings was relatively small, representing 4 percent, 7 percent, and 7 percent of the market value of the total stock of the respective companies. Common stock was offered to employees slightly more frequently than preferred stock. Occasionally companies sold employees special, nonvoting stock with fixed dividends. Many companies established length-of-service requirements for participating in stock ownership plans. National Cash Register employees received one share of common stock at the end of each of four successive years if their annual earnings were a thousand dollars or less, two shares if their earnings were greater than a thousand dollars. During this period, George Eastman is reputed to have made the largest single gift of stock to employees when he donated one million dollars of his personal holdings in the Eastman Kodak Company in 1919. Stock was often sold to employees at less

23. *Industrial Pension Systems*, vol. 2, p. 896.
24. *Management Review* 8, no. 9 (1921), p. 385.
25. "Employee Stock Ownership," *Encyclopaedia of Social Science*, p. 506.

than market price; if the market price was maintained, special financial advantages were often granted. Many companies provided for payment on an installment basis; others contributed directly to the purchase of stock. The Palmolive Company, Studebaker, and the Standard Oil companies matched employee contributions. When selling stock to employees was principally a means of raising capital, as was true of many public utilities, employee stock ownership did not constitute social policy. With respect to other possible benefits to the corporation, few employees bought large enough amounts of stock to inhibit their mobility if they found a better job elsewhere. And there is little evidence that stock ownership schemes reduced labor disputes.[26] In any case, the Wall Street Crash curtailed the development of such plans.

Many employee representation plans—also known as company unions, shop committees, work's councils, and industrial relations councils—were set up under the auspices of the National War Labor Board. After the First World War, independent management initiative became more important in establishing such plans. Between 1919 and 1922, 77 plans were terminated and 317 new ones established.[27] As table 2.1 shows, fewer plans existed in 1930 than in 1925, but the decline occurred mainly in smaller concerns. Usually employees elected their representatives, who then met with representatives of management. Some plans even had workers electing representatives to a "House" and a "Senate."

As a confidential adviser to John D. Rockefeller, Jr., Mackenzie King, the future prime minister of Canada, helped construct a number of employee representation plans, including one set up by the Colorado Fuel and Iron Company in the wake of events at Ludlow, Colorado, where women and children were among the victims when the National Guard set fire to strikers' tents. Under this plan, approved by about 80 percent of the workers, representatives were elected each year by secret ballot.[28] These representatives (one for

26. National Industrial Conference Board, *Employee Stock Purchase Plans in the United States* (New York, 1928), pp. 130–35.

27. National Industrial Conference Board, *Collective Bargaining through Employee Representation* (New York, 1933), p. 12.

28. F. A. McGregor, *The Fall and Rise of Mackenzie King, 1911–1919* (Toronto: Macmillan, 1962), pp. 182–83.

every 150 workers) met with management on a joint committee. King also advised the Bethlehem Shipbuilding Company, General Electric, International Harvester, and Standard Oil of Indiana on representation schemes. These plans showed that management was willing to make the ideological concession that workers had collective, not just individual, interests, although these interests were expressed through a representational structure approved by management, rather than independent institutions like trade unions. A 1923 survey of eighty plans categorized their effect on the division of management functions. While "managerial and business policies" remained almost entirely a management prerogative, wages, hours, working conditions, and the adjustment of grievances were generally the joint responsibility of employees and managers under these plans. Yet it appears that the employees' role in these areas was more often advisory than decisive, for in the category of "final decision," management alone had responsibility in more than 50 percent of the companies.[29] Some proponents claimed that representation materially benefited employees. For example, the eight-hour day in the steel works of the Colorado Fuel and Iron Company resulted from an "urgent request" on the part of employee representatives.[30] Others argued that employee representation plans were simply a cynical ploy on the part of management to thwart unionization. We will return to this issue in discussing the relationship between unionization and corporate social policies.

In 1929 about 22 percent of the money raised by 129 community chests was contributed by corporations. Since 1920, corporate contributions had increased from $2,535,819 to $12,954,769, paralleling the spread of community chests across the United States in the 1920s. A survey of thirteen chests found that the number of contributions from corporations almost doubled between 1920 and 1929.[31] The depression of 1921 stalled corporate giving, along with other corporate social policies. Individual corporations spread their

29. *System* 45 (January 1924), p. 44.

30. Ernest Burton, *Employee Representation* (Baltimore: Williams and Wilkins, 1926), p. 232.

31. Pierce Williams and Frederick Croxton, *Corporation Contributions to Organized Community Welfare Services* (New York: National Bureau of Economic Research, 1930), p. 11.

contributions widely—one gave to ninety-nine different community chests—but they tended to give most generously in cities where they conducted business. Aside from community chests, the YMCA was the chief beneficiary of corporate philanthropy. In 1917 more than one hundred YMCAs were supported jointly by employers and employees.[32] Five hundred lump-sum gifts of one million dollars or more were made to various charities in 1928. What Richard H. Bremner calls "the charitable zeal of business leaders" is all the more remarkable in that corporate charity was not tax exempt until 1935.[33]

One of the more interesting areas of corporate social policy during this period was the effort of businessmen to address the problem of unemployment. By 1934 twenty-three company schemes had been established to provide financially for the unemployed, and sixteen were still functioning. Five joint company-union schemes were also in operation, out of twenty-six that had been established. In 1931, 65,000 employees were covered by joint schemes and another 50,000 by company plans.[34] Although unions in Europe had had elaborate unemployment benefit schemes since before the turn of the century, American unions showed very little interest in developing such schemes for their members. It was business, not labor, that took the initiative in America. Most company plans paid unemployment benefits for a specified period. General Electric, financed by joint employer and employee contributions, paid half of the worker's normal earnings for ten weeks for each year of employment, provided he had served at least one year. The Leeds and Northrup Company plan paid 75 percent of normal wages to unemployed workers with dependents—an exceptionally high figure, even in comparison to past and present public-sector schemes. More than half of the unemployment benefit plans established during this period were noncontributory, that is, financed by the employer alone. In Rochester, New York, Eastman Kodak, Bausch and Lomb Optical Company, and seventeen other companies established

32. Ibid., p. 52.

33. *American Philanthropy* (Chicago: University of Chicago Press, 1960), p. 141.

34. *Monthly Labor Review* 38 (January 1934), p. 1,288.

a joint unemployment benefit plan. Five companies guaranteed employment for a certain number of weeks in the year. The remarkable Columbia Conserve Company of Indianapolis assured its employees of full pay for fifty-two weeks a year, while Proctor and Gamble guaranteed forty-eight weeks at full pay for its hourly factory workers.[35] Other companies paid dismissal compensation. Of the approximately 212 companies that reported doing so in 1934, some made flat payments, while others based compensation on length of employment. A week's pay for each year's service was the policy of fifteen companies.[36]

Preventing unemployment by "regularizing" production became popular in the 1920s. In 1931 it was estimated that more than two hundred companies were attempting to stabilize employment by manufacturing for stock, doing repairs, building plants, and cleaning when business was slow. As a result, unemployment in some industries reportedly declined. The costs of operating unemployment benefit schemes provided further incentives for employers to regularize production.[37] Gerard Swope of General Electric advocated organizing the large firms in each industry to stabilize production; the most successful would be exempt from paying into the companies' unemployment insurance fund. Although the Federal Trade Commission was to supervise the scheme, critics charged that it would violate antitrust policy by allowing firms to exchange information on production, inventories, and prices in order to stabilize production.

Regularizing production, controlling seasonal fluctuations in employment, and insuring employees against the hardships of unemployment were important elements of corporate social policy during this period. They illustrate the range of problems that businessmen felt they had the power to influence and for which they were willing to make themselves responsible. They also demonstrate how the private sector can successfully preempt the public

35. National Industrial Conference Board, *Essentials of a Program of Unemployment Reserves* (New York, 1933), Appendix A.

36. *Monthly Labor Review* 39 (November 1934), p. 1,067.

37. Bryce M. Stewart, *Unemployment Benefits in the United States* (New York: Industrial Relations Counsellors, 1930), p. 67; Julius Barnes, "Business Looks at Unemployment," *Atlantic Monthly,* August 1931, p. 244.

sector in a policy area. By claiming that they could successfully address social problems, businessmen allowed the federal government to defer making its own social policy until the Social Security Act was passed in 1935. A Senate committee investigating the problem of unemployment in 1929 concluded that private employers rather than government should provide unemployment benefits. The committee preferred to draw on American business experience, rather than copy "the systems of unemployment insurance now in vogue under foreign governments."[38] (Many European governments had started public-sector social welfare programs before World War I.)

Another element in the business solution to unemployment was high wages. Ford's sensational announcement of the five-dollar work day marked the development of a new attitude that became "respectable, even orthodox" in the 1920s, despite the fact that "the idea of paying more for labor than they had to pay was inconsistent with the whole habit of thought of the capitalist group."[39] High wages, through their effect on demand, would maintain employment at a high level. The practical effects of this change in attitude are difficult to ascertain. Generally speaking, wages were highest at the beginning of the decade, when the effects of the war were still being felt on the labor market. They dropped precipitously in the depression of 1921 but gradually increased, in real terms, throughout the 1920s, although they never quite regained their 1920 level. At the same time the length of the average industrial work week did decrease.[40] Further, for much of the decade unemployment was over 10 percent, so it is surprising in this context that there was any increase in wages, unless one looks at the attitudes of businessmen.

Factory-based medical care took off in the first three decades of the century. A 1926 survey of 430 companies conducted by the Bureau of Labor Statistics revealed that 373 companies had hos-

38. *Senate Report No. 2072*, 70th Cong., 2d sess., 1929, p. xi.

39. John R. Commons, *History of Labor in the United States, 1896–1932*, vol. 3 (New York: Macmillan, 1935), p. 91.

40. National Industrial Conference Board, *Wages, Hours and Employment in the United States, 1914–1936* (New York, 1936); Donald R. McCoy, *Coming of Age* (Harmonsworth, Middlesex: Penguin Books, 1973), p. 116.

pitals or emergency rooms and 311 actually employed a doctor. About 300 companies gave free medical care to employees. A few companies also provided treatment for workers' dependents. More than 80 firms employed full- or part-time dentists, and 32 employed eye specialists. It was also common "in quite a number of industries" to give poorly fed employees milk twice a day.[41] A National Industrial Conference Board study attributed the development of medical care during this period to pressure put on the employer from the enactment of factory inspection and workers' compensation laws, but also in part to "the growing personal interest of employers in the welfare of their employees."[42] In addition, approximately 280 firms offered free legal advice to employees in 1926. One company's legal staff prepared legal documents and represented employees in court, if necessary.

Employees' spare time did not escape the attention of corporate social policy makers. For a start, they provided more of it. Only 16 companies gave vacations with pay in 1916, compared to 133 ten years later. Athletic programs became common in the 1920s. In the 1926 survey, 319 companies reported that they had facilities for outdoor recreation, baseball being the most popular company game. Employers also sponsored indoor recreation of various kinds by providing gymnasiums, swimming pools, clubhouses, lectures, movies, or concerts, or helping to maintain company bands, orchestras, or glee clubs.

Employees profited from corporate social policy in mind as well as body. In 1926, 127 companies had libraries; the larger ones were open to the public as well as to employees. Besides keeping a watchful eye to ensure that books were suitable for employees, companies developed their own literature. The first employee magazine was the National Cash Register's *Factory News*, begun in 1890. But it was not until after the First World War that such publications became widespread. Of 334 employee magazines studied in 1921, when the depression temporarily halted their growth, more than 90

41. U.S. Bureau of Labor Statistics, "Health and Recreation in Industrial Establishments, 1926," *Bulletin no. 458* (Washington, D.C.: U.S. Government Printing Office, 1928), pp. 4–9.
42. *Medical Care of Industrial Workers* (New York, 1926), p. v.

percent were started between 1917 and 1920. Most of these magazines were published monthly and distributed free to employees.
Typically they contained inspirational articles, humor, articles on
plant processes and safety, personal items, and editorials on such
subjects as loyalty, thrift, and the prevention of waste. The magazines were designed to develop a feeling of cooperation among employees, foster pride in workmanship, and promote company loyalty.[43] Many corporations also established schools, where English,
mathematics, citizenship, and science were taught, in addition to
specific training programs.[44] The National Association of Corporation Schools, founded in 1913, included among its members AT&T,
Burroughs Adding Machines, Cadillac Motor Car Company, and
Commonwealth Edison. By the 1920s, then, there were educational,
legal, medical, recreational, and financial dimensions to corporate
social policy.

It is sometimes observed that corporations are immortal in that
they have a legal existence independent of individuals. But few are
willing to go as far as Allan Nevins when he claims that between
1914 and 1920 the Ford Motor Company "had a soul."[45] At least
towards the end of this period Nevins could have made a similar
claim for many large American corporations. Social policies associated with large corporations developed rapidly in the second decade of the century and peaked in the 1920s. The development of
corporate social policies over time shows their sensitivity to the
business cycle. The depression of 1921 interrupted the growth of
these policies and the Great Depression ended many of them, at
least in the form they had assumed in the 1920s. The 1930s revealed
to businessmen the magnitude of the responsibilities that they had
happily shouldered in prosperous times. The state came to their
relief with the passage of the Social Security Act in 1935. Nevertheless, businessmen's attitudes were perceptibly shifting towards
more social concern and greater sensitivity to public opinion.

43. National Industrial Conference Board, *Employee Magazines in the United
States* (New York, 1925).

44. Berenice M. Fisher, *Industrial Education* (Madison: University of Wisconsin Press, 1967), pp. 110–13.

45. *Ford*, vol. 1, p. 563.

three

Managerial Theory and
Corporate Social Responsibility

The growing number of stockholders, and the apparent willingness of some large stockholders not to take an active role in management, make professional managers increasingly dominant in the control and operation of the modern corporation. According to managerial theory, this displacement of stockholders by managers means that other motivations are guiding the corporation. Thus, corporate social responsibility and the policies described in the previous chapter may be a consequence of the rise of the modern corporation under managerial control.

The separation of ownership from control and its effects on business policy are issues that have occupied the most distinguished economists since the eighteenth century. Discussing joint stock companies, Adam Smith said of those who manage "other people's money" that "it cannot well be expected, that they should watch over it with the same anxious vigilance" as their own.[1] In volume 3 of *Capital*, Karl Marx briefly discusses the separation of ownership from control. Some have claimed this discussion as support for the doctrine of managerialism, while others maintain that Marx's point is to note an organizational change that is a development, not a transformation, of capitalist economic and social rela-

---

1. *An Inquiry into the Nature and Causes of the Wealth of Nations* (1776; reprint, Chicago: University of Chicago Press, 1976), vol. 2, p. 264.

tions.[2] Thorstein Veblen recognized a division of interest between the owners of business enterprises and the industrial experts who ran them, though he saw ownership interests as still dominant. Owners direct "the industrial experts" for their own commercial gain, Veblen wrote; expertise, not capital, should assert its right to control. Veblen invoked this new industrial order with his slogan "A Soviet of Technicians."[3] Keynes, in his essay "The End of Laissez-Faire," noted the division between shareholding and managing in large firms and discussed managers' motives as a managerial theorist might. His contemporary, Walther Rathenau, recognized the subdivision of corporate ownership and argued that among "the chiefs of the great corporate undertakings . . . we already encounter an official idealism identical with that which prevails in the state service . . . Covetousness, as the motive force, has been completely superseded by the sense of responsibility."[4]

Prescient Europeans apart, it was the work of Adolf Berle and Gardiner Means that caught the imagination of American social scientists. *The Modern Corporation and Private Property* (1932) was the first full-length effort to systematically study the issue of the separation of ownership from control. This work is of central interest here not only because it was written within the corporate context of the 1920s, but also because the authors' methods, findings, and hypotheses remain influential.

It is on the expansion and dispersal of stock ownership—the number of stockholders in the United States doubled between 1918 and 1925—that the claim of a separation of ownership from control rests and the edifice of managerialism is constructed. Berle and Means argue that in aggregating their wealth with that of numerous others, shareholders lose their power to control the firm's physical

---

2. See Ralf Dahrendorf, *Class and Class Conflict in Industrial Society* (Stanford: Stanford University Press, 1959) and Maurice Zeitlin, "Corporate Ownership and Control: The Large Corporation and the Capitalist Class," *American Journal of Sociology* 79 (March 1974).

3. *The Engineers and the Price System* (New York: Viking, 1921), p. 138.

4. *In Days to Come* (New York: Alfred A. Knopf, 1921) pp. 122–23.

assets and become "merely recipients of the wages of capital."[5] This development breaks down the old concept of property, in which the proceeds of wealth and control over its use were combined. According to Berle and Means, the locus of control within most corporations lies with those who select the board of directors. Formally, this power is exercised by stockholders who elect the directors annually. But with an increasing number of stockholders and a diminishing size of individual holdings, stockholders become progressively disenfranchised. Unless they own a lot of stock, their votes will not mean much; many do not vote at all or surrender their votes to the proxy committee selected by the existing management. Where stock is widely dispersed, ownership of a small percentage (nowadays put as low as 5 or 10 percent, though Berle and Means calculated 20 percent) can provide working control of a corporation. In this case the majority of stockholders have been separated from control of the corporation. The process is completed when even such minority holdings disappear and management, through proxy voting, becomes a "self-perpetuating body."[6] The American Telephone and Telegraph Company was, for Berle and Means, the institutional archetype of this corporate evolution, the bright future of managerial control. "Property worth hundreds of millions of dollars, belonging to tens or even hundreds of thousands of individuals, is combined through the corporate mechanism into a single producing organization under unified control and management."[7] Berle and Means viewed this organizational change as tremendously significant, altering the nature of capitalism itself. "This dissolution of the atom of property destroys the very foundation on which the economic order of the past three centuries has rested."[8]

Empirically, Berle and Means's argument was based on an analysis of the largest two hundred American nonfinancial corporations, ranked according to assets. They categorized 44 percent of these corporations as under management control at the beginning

5. *The Modern Corporation and Private Property* (New York: Macmillan, 1932), p. 3.

6. Ibid., p. 87.

7. Ibid., p. 3.

8. Ibid., p. 8.

of 1930. They claimed "reasonably definite and reliable information" on about two-thirds of the companies; for the rest they relied on newspaper reports or "street knowledge."[9] Maurice Zeitlin points out that they actually "had information which permitted them to classify as definitely under management control only 22 percent of the 200 largest corporations."[10] Lack of reliable information, coupled with a very conservative estimate of the percentage of stock ownership necessary for minority control (20 percent), may well have resulted in an overestimation of the extent of management control.

In the 1960s Robert Larner attempted to repeat Berle and Means's study. His definition of control—the power to select the board of directors—was the same as theirs, and he generally followed their procedures and classifications. But because of the increase in size of corporations and the wider dispersion of stock, Larner reduced the lower limit for minority control to 10 percent. In 1963, Larner claims, 84 percent of the two hundred largest nonfinancial corporations were controlled by management. In summary, says Larner, "it would appear that Berle and Means in 1929 were observing the so-called 'managerial revolution' in process. Thirty-four years later that 'revolution' seems close to complete."[11]

Coexistent with works like Larner's, which support the thesis of the separation of ownership and control as a dominant characteristic of the modern corporation, is an undercurrent of research muddying these social scientific waters. A Securities and Exchange Commission study, done for the Temporary National Economic Committee (TNEC) in the late 1930s, concluded that "ownership of voting stock remains the basic, the stablest, and the most secure vehicle of control."[12] Another significant finding of this study was that officers and directors held 6 percent of the common stock and about 2 percent of the preferred stock of the two hundred largest

9. Ibid., pp. 91–93.

10. "Corporate Ownership and Control," pp. 1,081–82.

11. *Management Control and the Large Corporation* (New York: Dunellen, 1971), p. 22.

12. *Investigation of Concentration of Economic Power*, Monograph no. 29 (Washington, D.C.: U.S. Government Printing Office, 1940), p. 7.

corporations.[13] While relatively small, the size in absolute terms of this stockholding may be sufficient to tie managerial interests to ownership interests, depending on what stock ownership represented in relation to other forms of managerial compensation.

In the early 1960s Don Villarejo looked at the 250 largest industrial corporations and concluded that from 54 to 61 percent were owner-controlled.[14] Also in the 1960s Robert Sheehan, using what he described as a conservative definition of control by putting the lower limit of minority ownership at 10 percent, found that in approximately 150 companies of the *Fortune* 500 controlling ownership was in the hands of an individual or a single family. Sheehan explained that he included neither "any of the various coalitions that may indeed assure working control for small groups of associates in many companies" nor "some businessmen known to wield great influence with holdings of less than 10 percent."[15] Jean-Marie Chevalier, in his study of control type in the two hundred largest nonfinancial corporations for 1965–66, found only eighty to be management-controlled. His definition of minority ownership was "liberal" in that he fixed the lower limit at 5 percent.[16] (Usually the attachment of a low percentage to minority control is justified by the example of, say, the Watson family at IBM, who own approximately 3 percent of the stock but have a controlling position.)

Critical of studies like Larner's that rely heavily on corporate reports to the Securities and Exchange Commission, which for a variety of reasons understate the concentration of stock ownership, Philip Burch systematically searched the business press as well as SEC reports from the period 1950 to 1971. In his study of the separation of ownership and control, he classified corporations on *Fortune*'s 1965 list as either management-controlled or family-controlled. His criteria for family control were that at least 4 to 5 percent of the stock was held by a family, a group of families, or an affluent

13. Ibid., p. xvi.

14. "Stock Ownership and the Control of Corporations," *New University Thought* (Autumn 1961–Winter 1962).

15. "Proprietors in the World of Big Business," *Fortune*, June 15, 1967, p. 180.

16. "The Problem of Control in Large American Corporations," *Antitrust Bulletin* 14 (Spring 1969), p. 166.

individual, and that there was inside or outside representation for the stockholding group on the board of directors, usually over an extended period of time. Burch found 58 percent of the fifty biggest industrial concerns, 43 percent of the top two hundred, and 41 percent of the top three hundred to be management-controlled.[17] Aware of the disparities between his study, the projections of Berle and Means, and the findings of Larner, Burch devotes his appendices to a reassessment of these studies and a critical discussion of their methods.

Also critical of the empirical foundation of managerialist theory, Maurice Zeitlin argues against accepting the separation of ownership and control as characteristic of corporations. Managerialists, according to Zeitlin, have underestimated the continuing importance of ownership in relation to control of the large corporation as a result of deficiencies in method and data collection. He suggests a case-by-case analysis sensitive to the interrelatedness of corporations and focusing on kinship patterns among top officers, directors, and the principal shareholders. He notes the understandable secrecy of large shareowners and their use of voting trusts, foundations, and holding companies as devices for holding stock. Through these and other devices, the "presence of principal proprietary families may be hidden or rendered scarcely noticeable among the reports of stock ownership filed with the Securities and Exchange Commission."[18] Zeitlin also points out that the customary use of the Fortune list to identify the largest corporations, there being no official list, means that privately owned companies that do not publish certified financial statements are left out. Approximately twenty-six such companies could have made the Fortune list in 1965, and therefore should have appeared in Larner's study.[19]

A British study corroborates the view that the separation of ownership and control has been overstated. It presents evidence on control in British industry "which shows that the extent of managerial control is more limited than has been thought and may not have an

17. The Managerial Revolution Reassessed (Lexington, Mass.: Lexington Books, 1972), p. 68.
18. "Corporate Ownership and Control," p. 1,086.
19. Ibid., p. 1,085.

inexorable tendency to increase."[20] Most recently the issue has been raised in Edward S. Herman's book *Corporate Control, Corporate Power.* Examining control type in the two hundred largest non-financial corporations in 1975, he classified 82.5 percent as management-controlled. The discrepancy between his figures and Burch's arises partly from their definitions of minority control. Herman presumes control whenever a party owns 10 percent or more of the stock, or "where a group demonstrably in control (usually the active managers) own five percent or more of the voting stock."[21] A large block of stock may be held by an individual or family who are not active in the management of the corporation, even though they may have some board representation. Herman regards this as a case of latent, as opposed to active, power and classifies it as a type of management control. So, for example, he counts Allied Chemical as management-controlled, although the Solvay group held 9.7 percent of the stock and in 1967 appeared to engineer a change in the firm's management. Herman claims that this "management displacement occurred at a time of serious company malaise" and that Solvay needed the help of other family interests, the Meyers and Nichols.[22] Burch, on the other hand, classifies Allied Chemical as family-controlled. In cases where the holding is over 10 percent, coupled with board representation, Herman "tended to posit control."[23]

In his study Herman distinguishes between the mechanism and the locus, the "how" and the "who," of control. Particularly with relatively small stockholdings of 1 to 5 percent, he maintains that the stock is less important in terms of control than the stockholder's strategic position in the organization. However, those who exercise control by virtue of their strategic position may well have sizeable stockholdings. In 1975, for example, the 4.2 percent of R. J. Reynolds Industries stock held by its officers and directors was worth

20. Steve Nyman and Aubrey Silberston, "The Ownership and Control of Industry," *Oxford Economic Papers* 30 (March 1978), p. 74.

21. *Corporate Control, Corporate Power* (Cambridge: Cambridge University Press, 1981), p. 304.

22. Ibid., p. 21.

23. Ibid., p. 304.

$180 million.[24] Controllers, then, may have ownership interests; ownership in this sense is not separated from control, although it is not through ownership that control is obtained. Ownership, for Herman, constrains but does not control corporate policy in this case. Herman's subcategories make it possible to calculate the extent of "substantial ownership interests" on the part of managers and directors in the two hundred largest nonfinancial corporations. Approximately 37 percent do not separate ownership from control, even though the stockholding may not provide the mechanism of control.

Herman argues that the investments of commercial banks and other financial institutions, while large, are characterized by "passivity in voting behavior" and have not led to cases of financial dominance over nonfinancial corporations.[25] Consequently, these large blocks of stock do not show up in his classification scheme of power in corporations. But through other means, such as lending powers and the presence of bankers on corporate boards, Herman says that "significant influence by financial institutions was present in a substantial minority of large companies," usually operating as "a constraining and negative power short of ultimate authority."[26]

The distinction between constraint and control is essential to Herman's argument. "Literal control . . . means the power to make the key decisions of a company . . . The power to constrain is used to mean the power to limit certain decision choices, as in a ceiling on dollars that may be spent on new facilities . . . The two terms are not mutually exclusive."[27] Herman's distinction, in other words, does not always distinguish, though he identifies cases of financial constraint and places them in a subcategory of management control. Some 19 percent of the two hundred corporations are classified as subject to financial constraint. Herman develops a theory of "constrained managerial control of the large corporation," under which "ownership persists as a powerful influence and constraint on man-

24. *Ibid.*, p. 63.
25. Ibid., p. 161.
26. Ibid., p. 159.
27. Ibid., p. 19.

agerial ends and behavior."[28] What Herman calls constraint others call control, and the different results of their analyses partially reflect these conceptual differences.[29] The results of the various studies can be summarized as follows:

Percentage of Management-controlled Corporations

	Top 200	Top 250	Top 500
Berle and Means (1932)	44%	—	—
TNEC (1940)	30%	—	—
Villarejo (1960)	—	46%	—
Sheehan (1967)	—	—	70%
Chevalier (1969)	40%	—	—
Larner (1970)	84%	—	—
Burch (1972)	43%	—	—
Herman (1981)	83%	—	—

Variety, then, is the spice of empirical work on this question. It will remain so as long as there is disagreement over definitions and procedures. To hope for rhadamanthine standards of classification is unrealistic, as the issue of the separation of ownership and control is irretrievably political. The idea that corporations are changing by themselves, and that managers may no longer be singularly wedded to the profit motive, undermines traditional opposition to capitalism. Management control may be one of W. B. Gallie's "essentially contested concepts." If not a "pseudo fact," as Zeitlin suggests, the separation of ownership and control is certainly an elusive one.[30] The doubt that surrounds its nature and extent makes

28. Ibid., p. 15.

29. In 1979 David Kotz claimed that 35 percent of the two hundred largest nonfinancial corporations were under financial control ("The Significance of Bank Control over the Large Corporations," *Journal of Economic Issues* 13 [June 1979], p. 411).

30. "Essentially Contested Concepts," *Proceedings of the Aristotelian Society* 56 (1955–56), p. 169: According to Gallie, some conceptual disputes, "although not resolvable by argument of any kind, are nevertheless sustained by perfectly respectable arguments and evidence . . . There are concepts which are essentially contested, concepts the proper use of which inevitably involves endless disputes about their proper uses on the part of their users." The Zeitlin quote is from "Corporate Ownership and Control," p. 1,107.

managerialist theory problematic as an explanation of corporate social policy.

Setting aside this difficulty for the moment, the central behavioral proposition of managerialists is that managers' selfish interests in management-controlled firms differ from owners' selfish interests and will lead them to pursue goals other than profit maximization. Keynes anticipated much of the later discussion on this issue when he wrote:

> A point arrives in the growth of a big institution . . . at which the owners of the capital, i.e, the shareholders, are almost entirely dissociated from the management, with the result that the direct personal interest of the latter in the making of great profit becomes quite secondary. When this stage is reached, the general stability and reputation of the institution are more considered by the management than the maximum of profit for the shareholders. The shareholders must be satisfied by conventionally adequate dividends; but once this is secured, the direct interest of the management often consists in avoiding criticism from the public and from the customers of the concern.[31]

However, as I hope to show, the desire to avoid public criticism is characteristic of any large corporation as an attribute of its power, regardless of its control type. In a similar vein to Keynes, Berle and Means maintained that with the separation of ownership from control "the interests of owner and of ultimate manager may, and often do, diverge . . . New responsibilities towards the owners, the workers, the consumers, and the State thus rest upon the shoulders of those in control."[32] Claiming that managers' stock ownership was negligible, Berle and Means suggested that the way was clear for community interests to assert themselves. These interests were defined as "fair wages, security to employees, reasonable service to their public, and stabilization of business." Berle and Means even insisted that if the corporate system was to survive, management

---

31. *The Collected Writings of John Maynard Keynes*, vol. 9, p. 289.
32. *The Modern Corporation*, p. 6.

must develop into a "purely neutral technocracy balancing a variety of claims by various groups in the community and assigning to each a portion of the income stream on the basis of pubic policy rather than private cupidity."[33] The threats to corporate survival are not specified in *The Modern Corporation and Private Property*, but a continuing theme in Berle's later works is the importance of what he calls the "public consensus."[34] This public consensus, or "public opinion," channels managerial discretion in socially useful directions, preventing the corporation from becoming a "tyrannous institution."[35]

Berle and Means's view of managerial control as a neutral technocracy, at least potentially in the public service, is controversial. Their insight was to see the corporation as a political institution in need of legitimacy and sensitive to public opinion. But Berle considered public consensus an independent, external device which ensured that corporate actions did not conflict with community interests. The possibility of business ideology itself framing the public consensus and creating a circular flow of favorable values and ideas is not considered.

Since Berle and Means's work, others have argued that divergent patterns of behavior should be expected in owner-controlled and management-controlled firms. Ralf Dahrendorf says that the effect of separating ownership and control is to produce two sets of roles representing different outlooks toward the firm and its relationship to society. "Never has the imputation of a profit motive been further from the real motives of men than it is for modern bureaucratic managers."[36] John K. Galbraith sees corporate growth, measured in sales, as the primary goal of the modern managerial corporation.[37] Joseph Monsen, Jr., and Anthony Downs construct a more formal theory of managerial firms. They describe it as "really nothing more than the application of the self-interest axiom in traditional theory

33. Ibid., p. 356.

34. *Power without Property* (New York: Harcourt Brace, 1959), p. 90.

35. *The Twentieth Century Capitalist Revolution* (New York: Harcourt Brace, 1954), p. 54.

36. *Class and Class Conflict*, p. 46.

37. *The New Industrial State* (New York: Mentor, 1971), p. 174.

to a new type of firm: one in which ownership is separate from management."[38] Managers, in their view, attempt to maximize their own incomes instead of the firm's profits. They argue that managerial firms have larger expense accounts, are more cautious, and are likely to be more conciliatory in their relations with employees and the public. We have come some distance from Berle and Means's "purely neutral technocracy," and Monsen and Downs differ from Galbraith in their analysis of growth motivation. But each of these writers plays down the profit motive and concludes that management control is inherently more socially responsible than owner control.

Criticism of these theories splits along two intersecting levels of analysis. One fastens on individual motivations, the other on the imperatives of the market system. At the level of the individual, it is suggested that the managerialists have misinterpreted the self-interest of managers. Those whose authority is bureaucratic—that is, derived from their office or strategic position rather than property ownership—continue to hold stock. Since property-related interests constitute an important part of their earnings, "managements' ownership and ownership-based income is absolutely so large as to gear manager and owner interests together."[39] Some managerialists claim that growth is opposed to profit in the motivation of the rational corporate executive—a claim countered by the argument that growth can only be realized through profits.[40] Thus, managers' selfish interests are the same as those that owner-controllers are assumed to have. At the level of the market system, corporate policy cannot deviate significantly from the pursuit of profit without risking bankruptcy and possibly exposing the firm to takeover. It may also make it more difficult for the firm to raise capital. In short, managerial discretion is restricted both by the nature of the market system and by a framework of personal incentives to maximize profits.

38. "A Theory of Large Managerial Firms," *The Journal of Political Economy* 73 (June 1965), p. 225.

39. Herman, *Corporate Control, Corporate Power,* p. 94.

40. See Paul Baran and Paul Sweezy, *Monopoly Capital* (New York: Monthly Review Press, 1968), p. 39.

Fortunately, the discussion need not halt at this somewhat abstract stage, for a number of studies have attempted to measure the profit performance of firms subject to the different control types. Of twelve such studies published between 1968 and 1981, only five found a significant difference in profit performance between owner- and management-controlled firms; that is, only five supported managerialist expectations.[41] Edward Herman contends that Robert Larner's work does support managerialist theory, inasmuch as he finds some evidence that profitability varies with control type, but Larner's own assessment of his findings is that "management-controlled corporations seem to be just about as profit oriented as are owner-controlled corporations."[42] Although H. K. Radice finds a relationship between control type and profitability, he notes that "our hypothesis . . . was not confirmed completely: we cannot conclude that owner-controlled firms show a greater tendency to maximize profits."[43] One other study has examined business ideologies, in-

41. The five studies that support managerialist theory are: Kenneth Boudreaux, "Managerialism and Risk-Return Performance," *Southern Economic Journal* 39 (January 1973); R. Joseph Monsen, Jr., John S. Chiu, and David E. Cooley, "The Effect of Separation of Ownership and Control on the Performance of the Large Firm," *Quarterly Journal of Economics* 82 (August 1968); John Palmer, "The Profit-Performance Effects of the Separation of Ownership from Control in Large U.S. Industrial Corporations," *The Bell Journal of Economic and Management Science* 4 (Spring 1973); H. K. Radice, "Control Type, Profitability and Growth in Large Firms," *The Economic Journal* 81 (September 1971); Miron Stano, "Monopoly Power, Ownership Control, and Corporate Performance," *The Bell Journal of Economics* 7 (Autumn 1976). The studies that do not support managerialist theory are: J. W. Elliot, "Control, Size, Growth, and Financial Performance in the Firm," *Journal of Financial and Quantitative Analysis* 7 (January 1972); Herman, *Corporate Control, Corporate Power* (1981); Peter Holl, "Effect of Control Type on the Performance of the Firm in the U.K.," *Journal of Industrial Economics* 23 (June 1975); David Kamerschen, "The Influence of Ownership and Control on Profit Rates," *American Economic Review* 58 (June 1968); John Kania and John McKean, "Ownership, Control, and the Contemporary Corporation: A General Behavior Analysis," *Kyklos* 29, no. 2 (1976); Robert Larner, *Management Control and the Large Corporation* (1970); Robert Sorenson, "The Separation of Ownership and Control and Firm Performance: An Empirical Analysis," *Southern Economic Journal* 41 (July 1974).

42. *Management Control,* p. 29.

43. "Control Type," p. 560–61.

stead of profit, in relation to control type and found no relationship;[44] management- and owner-controlled firms express the same ideology.

The evidence presented in these studies gives little reason for confidence that managerialist theory offers an explanation of corporate social responsibility. Confidence diminishes further when the hypothesized relationship between control type and social responsibility is examined directly using data from the 1920s. The analysis of this data provides additional evidence that control type has no significant effect on corporate behavior.

Data on control type for the 1920s is available from the Berle and Means study. Their classification of the largest two hundred nonfinancial corporations according to ultimate control provides information for 1929. Some firms were classified as controlled by "legal device," an intermediary category between minority ownership control and management control. Where this classification occurred, I used Philip Burch's evaluation of control type in his reassessment of Berle and Means's study (approximately one-fifth of the firms). For the purposes of this analysis, four separate types of social policy are identified: pension schemes, life insurance schemes, employee stock ownership schemes, and contributions to charity. Out of a total of 197 corporations (excluding three classified as "special situations" by Berle and Means), 111 are identified as having social policy. Of these, 77 had pension schemes, 11 had life insurance schemes, 69 had employee stock ownership schemes, and 40 contributed to charity.[45] I selected these types of social policy primarily because information identifying individual firms that practiced them was available. The data on pension and employee

44. Maynard Seider, "Corporate Ownership, Control and Ideology: Support for Behavioural Similarity," *Sociology and Social Research* 62 (October 1977), p. 123.

45. *Industrial Pension Systems*, vol. 2, Appendices A–C; National Industrial Conference Board, *Industrial Group Insurance* (1929), pp. 44–46; National Industrial Conference Board, *Employee Stock Purchase Plans in the United States* (1928), Appendix 25; Williams and Croxton, *Corporate Contributions*, Appendix. I would like to thank the Data Lab of the Department of Political Science, Indiana University, for help with this section.

Table 3.1   Control Type and Social Policy in Top 200 U.S. Firms, 1929

	Management control	Ownership control
No social policy	38%	51%
Social policy	62%	49%
	100%	100%
	(N = 112)	(N = 85)

Chi-square = 2.4 with 1df. not significant at the 0.05 level
Gamma = −0.24

stock ownership is most complete, based as it is on comprehensive surveys of American industry at the time. For life insurance schemes only a selected list of firms was available, but this selection was not influenced by control type. Contributions to charity were identified from a list of contributors to a Red Cross war fund.

It is possible that more of the 197 corporations, both owner- and management-controlled, had social policy than is indicated in this analysis. For, for example, is not included among owner-controlled companies that had social policy, although, as we have seen, it raised wages and introduced the eight-hour work day as early as 1914. But there is no reason to suppose that additional data on other types of social policy would lead to a different conclusion. Although the existence of any one of the four types listed above is sufficient for the corporation to be classified as having social policy, more than half the corporations surveyed engaged in more than one type. The fit between the date of information on control type (1929) and the dates of information on social policy is not exact. The chronological gap is least with pensions (1929) and greatest with charity (1918). Any resulting distortion should favor managerialist expectations, if the managerialist claim of a trend toward management control is correct. Table 3.1 shows that more management-controlled firms have social policy than owner-controlled firms. But the 13 percent difference provides poor support for managerialist theory. There is no significant relationship between type of control and the presence or absence of social policy. That is, the gamma (-0.24) suggests that there is only a weak relationship, and the low

Table 3.2 Size, Control Type, and Social Policy in Top 200 U.S. Firms, 1929

	Small		Medium		Large	
	M	O	M	O	M	O
No social policy	42%	60%	35%	46%	41%	30%
Social policy	58%	41%	65%	55%	60%	70%
	100%	101%	100%	101%	101%	100%
	(N = 24)	(N = 42)	(N = 51)	(N = 33)	(N = 37)	(N = 10)

Sources: See n. 45.
Note: M = management-controlled; O = owner-controlled. Percentages may not total 100 due to rounding error. Three firms classified by Berle and Means as "special situations" are excluded from this analysis.

chi-square (2.4) indicates that even that relationship is not statistically significant.

However, there is considerable variation in size among the largest two hundred American corporations on which this analysis is based. Size is interesting both because it is expected to influence control type—larger firms are more likely to have a wider distribution of stockholdings and are more likely to be management-controlled—and because it might also be taken as an indication of the capacity to produce social policy. Using Berle and Means's figures on size as measured by assets, the firms can be placed in three categories: small (up to $160 million), medium ($161 to $500 million), and large (over $500 million). As shown in table 3.2, differences in size appear to influence control type and, to an extent, the existence of social policy. In general, the larger the firm the likelier it was to be management-controlled and to have social policy. The 36 percent of small firms that were management-controlled rose to 61 percent in the medium category and 79 percent in the large category. Forty-seven percent of small firms had social policy, compared to 61 percent of medium-size firms and 62 percent of large firms. Interestingly, as size increases any relationship between control type and social policy disappears. The data shows that the largest owner-controlled firms were slightly more likely (by 70 percent to 60 percent) to have social policy than management-controlled firms. Size, as related to market power, may be important because it influences both the ability of firms to provide social policy and the existence of legitimacy problems that may encourage the formulation of such policy.

Whether the separation of ownership from control in the modern corporation can account for social policy, as various managerial theories might lead us to expect, is open to question. A review of research on the extent of this separation reveals a considerable variation in findings. Herman's influential book *Corporate Control, Corporate Power* (1981) categorizes more than 80 percent of the two hundred largest American corporations as management-controlled. This accords with Berle and Means's suggested trend toward managerial control. But Herman's study robs the observation of the separation of ownership from control of much of its behavioral significance by developing a theory of "constrained managerial control," under which ownership remains a powerful influence in managerial decisionmaking. Much of the empirical work on the implications of the separation of ownership from control has not supported managerialist theory. The data from the 1920s does not indicate any strong association between the making of social policy and managerial control. Rather, it reveals that large firms are likely to make social policy, irrespective of control type.

four

Unions and Corporate
Social Responsibility

Dissatisfaction with the theory of managerialism leads us to a second plausible and indeed popular explanation of corporate social policies in the 1920s. In this view, these policies represented simply another anti-union device in the employers' repertoire. "The central purpose of welfare capitalism," Irving Bernstein writes, was "avoidance of trade unionism."[1] Similarly, Stuart Brandes argues that "at its heart, welfare capitalism was a defensive strategy. Particularly after World War I, it was a protective device aimed largely at trade unionism."[2]

It must be conceded that business social policies constituted a fundamental threat to unionism. Insofar as these policies justified the corporation to its workers, they undermined the presumption of a separate worker self-interest on which unionism rested. The national parallel for this process is the development of the welfare state and its effect on the propensity to make revolution. It is a commonplace of left-wing criticism that state welfare policies "buy off" worker dissent and delay the process of social transformation. Yet there are both Bismarcks, who see welfare policies as ultimately preempting socialist demands, and Beveridges, who see these policies as solutions to social problems. While the effect of the policies may be similar, the intentions behind them differ.

1. *The Lean Years* (Baltimore: Penguin, 1966), p. 187.
2. *American Welfare Capitalism* (Chicago: University of Chicago Press, 1976), p. 32.

Those who support the view of corporate social policy as an anti-union device rely largely on a comparison of corporate social policy development with the power of the labor movement and unions. According to Brandes, corporate social policies in the first decade of the twentieth century were initiated and expanded "in step with the rising level of labor militancy."[3] As labor became more aggressive, he implies, corporations responded with various social policies directed at employees' welfare. He offers a similar explanation for the increase in corporate social policy in the 1920s. "The anti-union overtones of welfare were clear and definite. An important indicator is the parallel expansion and contraction of welfare and union activities; welfarism rose and fell concordantly with unionism. The spurt in welfare programs during the 1920s was in part a response to the gains made by organized labor during World War I."[4] But Brandes's use of the words *parallel* and *concordantly* is misleading. In fact, he himself notes the time interval between the labor movement of the war years and social policy developments of the 1920s. A third version of his argument describes an inverse relationship between social policy and the labor movement. "Because of the clear evidence of lessening labor militancy at a time when welfare capitalism was on the rise, it would indeed be very difficult to argue that welfarism did not play a part."[5] Brandes implies that the increase in corporate social policies brought about a decline in labor militancy and that we should explain the policies in terms of this decline.

An empirical assessment of this argument starts with the state of the labor movement in the twenties. One indicator of union strength is membership. As the following table shows, union membership peaked in 1920, plunged in the next three years, and continued to decline for the rest of the decade, apart from a small gain in 1927.[6] So the increase in social policies during the 1920s did

3. Ibid., p. 19.
4. Ibid., p. 32.
5. Ibid., p. 136.
6. Leo Wolman, *Ebb and Flow in Trade Unionism* (New York: Bureau of Economic Research, 1936), p. 16.

Year	Membership	Year	Membership
1915	2,582,600	1923	3,622,000
1916	2,772,700	1924	3,536,100
1917	3,061,400	1925	3,519,400
1918	3,467,300	1926	3,502,400
1919	4,125,200	1927	3,546,500
1920	5,047,800	1928	3,479,800
1921	4,781,300	1929	3,442,600
1922	4,027,400	1930	3,392,800

indeed coincide with a decline in union strength. However, the plunge in union membership in 1921–22 was accompanied by significant cutbacks in corporate social policies. Since both of these developments can be attributed to a third factor, the depression, it is unlikely that the period of greatest union decline resulted from corporate social policy.

Despite the image of prosperity, the twenties generally were a time of high unemployment. It has been estimated that unemployment was 13 percent in 1924 and never dropped below 10 percent for the rest of the decade.[7] The influx of people from rural to urban areas compensated for a slower rate of immigration in maintaining a pool of surplus labor during this period. There was also a significant increase in the number of women in the work force at this time. As might be expected, labor turnover was low. Strike activity decreased along with union membership. The number of strikes in 1926 was less than a third of what it had been in 1919.[8] These conditions put employers in a powerful position in relation to labor.

Indeed, it is possible to argue that employers had little reason to be worried about the labor movement, no need to "buy off" workers, and therefore no incentive to pursue social policy principally as an anti-union device. While the labor market remained favorable, social policy effort actually increased, among both unionized and nonunionized corporations.[9] Most of the companies included in a

7. Bernstein, *The Lean Years*, p. 59.
8. Sumner Slichter, "The Current Labor Policies of American Industries," *Quarterly Journal of Economics* 43 (May 1929), pp. 396–97 and 428.
9. Ibid., p. 397.

National Industrial Conference Board survey of employee stock ownership schemes reported that they had never had any labor disputes.[10] Murray Latimer, in his study of corporate pension policies, says that apart from the railroad "those industries in which most of the workers covered by pension systems are engaged have never been strongly organized." With respect to the railroads, the expansion in pension plans coincided with the expansion in union membership.[11] In sum, the evidence does not support the argument that social policies were principally an anti-union device. Even if corporate policy makers were motivated by an irrational fear of unionization, this fear could be expected to diminish as the decade wore on.

A better explanation of union development would focus not on what employers did in terms of social policies, but on what unions did not do. American unions, in contrast to their counterparts in Europe, did not develop elaborate benefit systems. The importance of these systems is that they provided "selective incentives" in Mancur Olson's sense, for belonging to a union. It may be difficult for unions to restrict to their members the benefits of a wage rise that they have fought for, but they can exclude nonmembers from union benefits. While it was common practice for European unions to pay unemployment benefits to their members, American unions spent only $120,770 on such benefits in 1916. By contrast, British unions spent $6,289,565 on the unemployed in 1908.[12] As early as 1901 the Belgian city of Ghent began to subsidize union unemployment benefit schemes. European governments generally began public-sector unemployment provisions by contributing to existing union schemes, modeled on the Ghent system, thus increasing the incentive to join or remain in unions. Unemployment benefits provided incentives to remain a union member during depressions, when union membership tends to erode faster.

It is tempting to speculate that the development of company benefit schemes may have preempted the development of union schemes,

10. *Employee Stock Purchase Plans in the U.S.*, p. 131.

11. *Industrial Pension Systems*, vol. 2, p. 759.

12. David Smelser, *Unemployment and American Trade Unions* (Baltimore: Johns Hopkins University Press, 1919), p. 130.

and thus indirectly contributed to the difficulties of American unions. However, American unions showed little inclination to develop these activities even before the company schemes were established, and foreign unions had been heavily involved with benefit programs since at least the turn of the century. Rather, the "slight development of the out-of-work benefit in American trade unions" is immediately attributable to a reluctance to pay higher dues and inadequate union administrative structures.[13]

The reactions of labor leaders to corporate social policies are pertinent to the discussion of the role that anti-unionism played in the formation of these policies. From labor leaders' reactions it is possible to draw inferences about the strategy behind the policies. Brandes claims that "labor leaders of the 1920s to a man disliked welfarism and clearly hated employee representation."[14] This is an overstatement. In word and deed union leaders betrayed some ambivalence toward corporate social policy, excepting employee representation. A 1924 editorial in the *American Federationist* entitled "Mr. Swope sees the Light" commended Gerard Swope—the president of General Electric and a leading advocate of corporate social policies—for his support of high wages. According to the editorial, "Organized labor is seeing its educational work bear fruit not only in the ranks of workers, but also in the ranks of those who too often regard themselves as opponents of labor."[15] In 1927 the paper again praised Swope for the principles underlying his approach to management. "These principles reflect an industrial philosophy of unusual penetration and balance. They fall into four groups: responsibility to the consuming public, to its employees, to its stockholders and for its own perpetuation."[16]

William Green, president of the American Federation of Labor,

13. Ibid., p. 146. For a development of this argument, see Norman Furniss and Neil J. Mitchell, "American Exceptionalism in Comparative Perspective" (Paper presented at the Fifth Conference of Europeanists, Washington, D.C., 1985).

14. *American Welfare Capitalism*, p. 138.

15. *American Federationist* 31 (July 1924), p. 574.

16. "Cooperation—A Responsibility of Industry," *American Federationist* 34 (April 1927), p. 403.

himself used the language of the corporate social policy makers when he wrote that "the antagonistic and hostile attitude, so characteristic of the old order in industry, must be supplanted by a friendly relationship and a sense of obligation and responsibility."[17] Corporate social policy makers commonly described their efforts as contributing to harmony and cooperation in industry; Green's "modern trade unionism" shared these values. According to J. W. Sullivan of the Typographical Union, trade unionists viewed the National Civic Federation's efforts to promote corporate social policy with sympathy because the federation "promoted specific betterments for the working classes, supplemented trade union endeavors, and carried out the good intentions of enlightened employers."[18] Arthur Schlesinger, Jr., says that the labor leadership in 1928 "could hardly have been less rebellious." He quotes John L. Lewis's description of Herbert Hoover, who was an active supporter of corporate social policy, as "the foremost industrial statesman of modern times."[19] The *American Federationist* even carried corporation advertisements for their social policies, which implies that unions did not consider these policies dangerous to their development.

As Brandes points out, however, labor leaders were consistently critical of employee representation schemes or company unions. These schemes clearly constituted an open challenge to trade unions. "It seems to me pretty evident," Green said, "that employee representation plans are consciously or unconsciously substitutes for trade unions."[20] Labor hostility persisted despite assurances from some employers and their spokesmen that these schemes were not to be seen as a substitute for unions. The President's Industrial Conference of 1920 suggested that if these schemes were considered an anti-union device, they could not be "a lasting agency of indus-

17. "The Problem which Modern Trade Unionism Confronts," *American Federationist* 32 (April 1925), p. 227.

18. Ibid., p. 272.

19. *The Crisis of the Old Order* (Boston: Houghton Mifflin, 1957), p. 113.

20. Ernest Burton, *Employee Representation* (Baltimore: Williams and Wilkins, 1926), p. 65.

trial peace."[21] But statements of this kind did not placate the labor movement. Employee representation schemes did not guarantee the protection for workers that a union could. Paul Douglas argued that employers, despite pledges to the contrary, often attempted to influence elections of worker representatives, that the representatives seldom discussed important issues, that representatives who took their responsibilities too seriously were sometimes intimidated by threats of dismissal, and that joint committees of managers and worker representatives in many cases did not have the power to make final decisions.[22]

Despite union hostility, some employers tried to involve unions in their schemes. Mackenzie King, one of the originators of such schemes, was pleased to learn that Bethlehem Steel Corporation had recognized the union within months of his negotiating with management.[23] According to the President's Industrial Conference, "In many plants the trade-union and the shop committee are both functioning harmoniously. In some establishments the men are unionized, and the shop committees are composed of union men."[24] At Standard Oil of New Jersey's Baton Rouge refinery, the members of the union voted unanimously to support the representation plan, according to Clarence Hicks.[25] A recent study by Daniel Nelson divides employee representation schemes into three categories, the third of which is described as the "backbone" of the company union movement in the 1920s. Calling these plans the "hallmark of advanced personnel management," Nelson argues that their purpose was not "the containment or the obfuscation of the workers' economic interests."[26]

A number of union-management agreements in the twenties ex-

21. "Report of the Industrial Conference called by the President," *Annual Report of the Department of Labor, 1920* (Washington, D.C.: U.S. Government Printing Office, 1921), p. 240.

22. "Shop Committees: Substitute for, or Supplement to Trade Unions," *The Journal of Political Economy* 29 (February 1921), pp. 94–95.

23. McGregor, *The Fall and Rise of Mackenzie King*, p. 253.

24. "Report of the Industrial Conference," p. 240.

25. *My Life*, p. 58.

26. "The Company Union Movement, 1900–1937: A Reexamination," *Business History Review* 56 (Autumn 1982), p. 357.

plicitly recognized the union as the legitimate representative of the workers. The most famous was the Baltimore & Ohio Railroad plan of 1923. Sir Henry Thornton, president of Canadian National Railways, said: "On the Canadian National Railway system we are definitely and irrevocably committed to the principle of cooperation with employees through their existing unions."[27] There were also instances of cooperation in the garment and textile industries, and the Rocky Mountain Fuel Company had an agreement with the miners' union.[28] Union reaction to corporate social policies makes it difficult to infer that they were primarily an anti-union device. Indeed, in view of the meekness of trade unions during this period, it is unlikely that unions posed, or were perceived to pose, a significant threat to employers. Unionism is a peripheral rather than central factor in explaining corporate social policy.

What, then, had happened to make unemployment and financial provision for old age problems for businessmen to solve? It has been noted that corporate social policies were chiefly associated with large firms. Edward Berkowitz and Kim McQuaid, who note this association in explaining why welfare capitalism, instead of a welfare state, developed in the United States in the 1920s say that welfare capitalism "was less the product of a conscious corporate conspiracy than it was testimony to the comparative organizational advantage the corporate sector held over the government."[29] But simply having the money or the bureaucratic capacity does not explain why the money was spent, or the organization used, in a particular way, as Berkowitz and McQuaid seem to suggest. Only by studying the intentions and beliefs of corporate policy-makers can we arrive at a fuller, more coherent account of policy formation. The development of social policy reflected a changed business ideology and a response to the general problem of corporate legitimacy. Insofar as unionism was a target of this policy, it is only by examining this ideology that we can understand why employers did not stick with the more routine repressive techniques of combating unionism.

27. "When Man and Management Get Together," *Factory and Industrial Management* 78 (December 1929), p. 1,372.

28. Bernstein, *The Lean Years*, pp. 99–100.

29. *Creating the Welfare State* (New York: Praeger, 1980), p. 160.

What is required is a systematic treatment of this new business ideology in its connection with social policy. This policy was not simply the product of a moment in history—although particular historical circumstances gave substance to the problem of corporate legitimacy and the solution chosen—but of a continuing dynamic. First, however, we need to lay out the theoretical framework that integrates ideology, policy, and legitimacy within the large corporation.

five

Corporations as Political Institutions

Just as the application of economic analysis has led to a fuller understanding of political institutions, so political science may lead to a fuller understanding of economic institutions. Social responsibility presents a problem for economists, and they are unlikely to be satisfied with sophistical explanations like "long-term profit." In this and subsequent chapters, I will develop the perspective of the corporation as a political institution and corporate social policy as the product of an ideology of business power. Both business firms and governments seek to legitimize their power through ideology and policy. The contradictory functions of capital accumulation and legitimation that James O'Connor finds in the contemporary capitalist state are also present in the modern large corporation. O'Connor, writing from a Marxist perspective, maintains that the state fosters capital accumulation, but at the same time has to ensure social acquiescence through welfare measures, which are a financial drain on the capital accumulation process.[1] Imagine the corporation as being subject to similar demands. The following dynamic is at work:

- The firm tries to make a profit.
- The firm seeks power in order to make and maintain a profit.
- This power requires legitimacy.
- The firm presents itself as pursuing the good of the community as a whole, often by denying, at least verbally, its profit-seeking function in order to legitimize its power.

1. *The Fiscal Crisis of the State* (New York: St. Martin's, 1973), p. 6.

Corporate social policy is the result of an ideology of business power that emphasizes social responsibility and is a response to threats to corporate legitimacy.

The concepts of profit, power, legitimacy, ideology, and policy, and the relationships among them, require elaboration. Profit, in this view, remains the dominant goal of the corporation and its officials. For several reasons, it is the chief criterion for the exercise of business power. Not only is profit the basis of managerial compensation, it remains a key element within the new ideology, though in combination with other goals. Moreover, profit is seen as a defense against bankruptcy or takeover, and profit and the likelihood of profit influence the cost of raising capital. As shown in chapter 2, social policy is a secondary objective that depends on the firm realizing its primary goal of profit—thus the sensitivity of corporate social policy to the business cycle.

In seeking profits, corporations accrue power which maintains and extends their profit-seeking activity. The Medici family's slogan underscores this reciprocity: "Money to get power, power to protect money."[2] Steven Lukes defines power as "human agents, separately or together, in groups or organizations, through action or inaction, significantly affecting the thoughts or actions of others."[3] Those affected by the corporation include employees, customers, suppliers, stockholders, and the community—city, state, and nation. (We are used to seeing political leaders at all levels courting individual corporations in hopes of influencing their investment policies and plant-location decisions.) The corporation's decisions immediately and significantly affect who works, how many work, the nature of work, the rewards of work, the future prospects for work, the physical environment of work, and the quality and safety of the product of work. The less competition, the more these decisions are taken by the individual firm; that is, as the firm approaches a monopoly position, its officials have greater discretion over supply, quality, and price. In a competitive market, on the other hand, these deci-

2. Quoted in Daniel R. Fusfield, "The Rise of the Corporate State in America," in Warren J. Samuels, ed., *The Economy as a System of Power* (New Brunswick, N.J.: Transaction Books, 1979), vol. 1, p. 153.

3. *Essays in Social Theory* (London: Macmillan, 1972), p. 6.

sions are not within the discretion of the individual firm but are the result of the aggregation of decisions of many firms, or market forces. Power is directly related to the degree that market forces are subject to management. The most important source of market power is "large size relative to the market: the situation in which a few large firms account for all or nearly all of supply."[4] The relationship between large size and social policies is supported by the pattern of corporate social policies in the 1920s, the analysis of control type and corporate social policy, and a number of other studies.[5]

A necessary condition for corporate social policy is the excess profit permitted by the possession of market power. In a competitive market, if a firm voluntarily incurs additional costs, its competitive position is endangered and it may go out of business. As Kaysen says, "Only the ability to earn a substantial surplus over costs makes possible a variety of expenditures whose benefits are broad, uncertain, and distant."[6] Of course, simply having the capacity to make social policy does not mean that excess profit will be used in this way, and higher profit will not necessarily increase a firm's social policy effort. Market power enables corporations to earn excess profits and provides management with the discretionary power to make policy choices that otherwise would be dictated by the market. At the same time, only if management has this power does it face problems of legitimacy—"the generally observable need of any power, or even of any advantage of life, to justify itself"—which social policy addresses.[7] In other words, the power that makes social policy possible also generates the need for it.

In the nineteenth century businessmen sought legitimacy in an ideology based on classical economic theory, the pivotal assump-

4. Carl Kaysen, "The Corporation: How Much Power? What Scope?," in Edward Mason, ed., *The Corporation in Modern Society* (Cambridge, Mass.: Harvard University Press, 1960), p. 89.

5. See Raymon J. Aldag and Kathryn M. Bartol, "Empirical Studies of Corporate Social Performance," in Lee E. Preston, ed., *Research on Corporate Social Performance and Policy* (Greenwich, Conn.: JAI, 1978).

6. "The Social Significance of the Modern Corporation," p. 314.

7. Max Weber, *Economy and Society* (New York: Bedminster, 1968), vol. 3, p. 953.

tion of which is competition. From this assumption comes the claim of powerlessness on the part of the individual firm. Power is located in the market system, not the firm; after all, we refer to the "forces" of the market. Under this ideology, the firm's activity in the competitive market is in harmony with the public good and thus is self-legitimizing. John K. Galbraith writes: "The market allows of private purpose because it keeps it aligned with public purpose. The market is an expression of public preference and desire. The firm responds to the market. The firm is under public control and the public cannot be in conflict with itself."[8]

Reflecting public preferences, accumulation, or profit-making, is legitimation. Those dissatisfied with an individual supplier do not tarry to question or criticize that supplier, they turn to a new one. If enough buyers "exit," the firm goes out of business. As the firm's product is subject to market forces, so are its employment practices. According to this ideology, economic misfortune for an employee— unemployment or poverty as a result of low wages—is also outside the control of an individual employer and is to be faced in the same way as a natural disaster; with resignation, not rebellion. Needless to say, the more competitive a firm's situation actually is, the more persuasive this ideology is likely to be and, indeed, the more the employer will have to rely on this sort of justification, because he does not have the discretion to do anything else. When faced with complaints or strikes, the employer's defense in a competitive market is to explain to his employees, or to regulatory authorities, that he is not responsible for low wages or poor working conditions and that he cannot deviate from industry norms and stay in business.

Only when power is recognized as a product of the rise of the modern corporation, and the equation of private interest and public good breaks down, do the business functions of accumulation and legitimation become contradictory. Further, in situations of oligopoly or monopoly, the limited number of suppliers means that "exit" is no longer a readily available option. Instead, those dissatisfied with a firm's performance attempt to change its practices or

8. "On the Economic Image of Corporate Enterprise," in Ralph Nader, ed., *Corporate Power in America* (New York: Grossman, 1973), p. 4.

policies by exercising their political"voice." As Albert O. Hirschman writes, "In the economic sphere, the theoretical construct of
pure monopoly would spell a no-exit situation, but the mixture of
monopolistic and competitive elements characteristic of most real
market situations should make it possible to observe the voice option in its interaction with the exit option."[9] "Voice" implies an
attempt on the part of dissatisfied individuals to change, rather than
escape, the practices or policies of an organization. The presence
of the "exit" option adds strength to "voice." For example, the boy-
cott is the principal weapon of the Reverend Jesse Jackson's "Operation Push," which attempts to persuade corporations to hire
minorities and buy from minority businesses. Hirschman's categories illuminate the political aspect of the corporation. As he says,
"Voice is nothing but a portion and function of any political system."[10] The ideological resolution to the problem of legitimizing the
power of the modern corporation is to shift from denying power to
actively justifying it—by denying selfishness. Corporate social policy is a result of this shift.

Legitimacy refers to the belief among groups within the affected
population—workers, consumers, stockholders, and managers themselves—that the exercise of power is justified. Power is at risk if
legitimacy is not established. Even firms like Dow, which sell their
products mainly to other companies rather than directly to the public, are sensitive to this problem. As Robert W. Lundeen, chairman
of Dow, recognizes, "We found that if we were perceived as not
running our business in the public interest, the public will get back
at us with restrictive regulations and laws."[11] As we have seen, the
railroads were the first corporations to be involved in social policies, in part because they were the first really large firms. They also
engendered significant public hostility and early faced the possibility of government regulation.

Problems of legitimacy are more or less severe according to the
number and range of groups who believe that the exercise of power

9. *Exit, Voice and Loyalty,* p. 33.
10. Ibid., p. 30.
11. Philip Shabecoff, "Dow Stoops to Calm Congress and Public Opinion,"
The New York Times, January 2, 1985, p. 38.

is unjustified. The level at which criticism is targeted—be it individual firms (Teddy Roosevelt's "malefactors of great wealth") or industries—is also an important factor. If criticism is directed at capital in general, attempts to justify the exercise of power by professing social responsibility and making social policy are likely to be fruitless. In other words, corporate social policy is most appropriate as a defense against nonsocialist criticism of corporations—that is, against those who are willing to make a distinction between "good" and "bad" corporations.

Although legitimacy may coincide with legality, it is not the same as legality. Law changes in response to specific questions of legitimacy. The Sherman Antitrust Act of the late nineteenth century can be interpreted as the state's response to public discontent with the concentration of capital and the rise of corporate power. The courts subsequently reconciled the act to the process of concentration. Thus, while exercises of power may technically fit the law, they are not necessarily legitimate as far as the community is concerned.

Legitimacy problems are addressed by ideology. In Marx's analysis, ideology intervenes between reality and a class's true appreciation of reality (consciousness), resulting in false consciousness.[12] Ideology is descriptive and explanatory but, as John Plamenatz says, "it need not be false."[13] While ideology expresses collective interests, not restricted to class, this does not in itself make ideological description or explanation wrong. There is an overt persuasive content to ideology, which may be more or less well grounded in reality. The "false consciousness" view best fits an ideology like Nazism, based as it is on the "big lie." In expressing group interests, ideology provides justification or legitimacy for group actions, as well as establishing a guide to conduct for members of groups. It offers arguments for, and explanations of, institutions and social relationships; in doing so it provides legitimacy. Ideology is not simply

12. Actually, "false consciousness" is Engels's phrase, although it accords with Marx's view of ideology and is commonly attributed to Marx. See Engels's letter to F. Mehring, July 14, 1893, in *Marx and Engels: Selected Works* (London: Lawrence and Wishart, 1970), p. 690.

13. *Ideology* (New York: Praeger, 1970), p. 79.

manufactured or dreamed up after the fact as a public relations exercise to mask the policy makers' real intentions. Ideology, by implying certain courses of action, may serve both to transform and to preserve social, political, and economic institutions and relationships. These functions are not dichotomous—preservation may entail at least partial transformation. Ideology is a system of ideas that gives intelligibility to social life, providing members of groups with purpose and a sense of social worth.

"Life," says Marx, "is not determined by consciousness, but consciousness by life."[14] Curiously, these words do not capture the dialectical nature of ideology; for the way that life is conceptualized also guides human action and influences social change, as the history of Marx's own ideas demonstrates. Other economists are very much aware of the wide significance of their intellectual formulations, even ones that are outmoded. "Practical men," says Keynes, are "the slaves of some defunct economist." In fact, ideology is distinguished from other systems of thought chiefly by its explicitly practical focus on the aims and rules of collective conduct, or on the use or prospective use of power. Within political science, Charles Anderson has attempted to reconnect policy to what men think and say.[15] The thrust of Anderson's work is to see policy as "conscious design" and not simply as the product of "environmental" factors like the level of industrialization, demography, or technological imperatives. Key to his approach to policy analysis is the importance given to the ideas and values of policy-makers. Only by attending to these and so rediscovering the intentions and strategies of policy-makers can we explain policy making, Anderson argues. The initial decision to describe a condition as a problem within the policy-making body's sphere of competence depends on the value framework of the policy-makers. The application of a set of standards, or what Anderson calls a "logic of evaluation," translates a

14. *The German Ideology* (London: Lawrence and Wishart, 1970), p. 47.
15. "System and Strategy in Comparative Policy Analysis," in W. B. Gwyn and G. C. Edwards, eds., *Perspectives on Public Policy Making* (New Orleans: Tulane University Press, 1975); "The Logic of Public Problems: Evaluation in Comparative Policy Research," in Douglas Ashford, ed., *Comparing Public Policies* (Beverly Hills, Cal.: Sage Publications, 1978).

condition into a problem: Chinese Marxists understand "overpopulation," Catholics do not. Ideologies are a type of logic of evaluation.

Corporate social policies are understandable if they are seen as an expression of a new ideology of business power that reflected a new logic of evaluation on the part of businessmen. Previously, the problems corporate social policy was to address—unemployment, low wages, poverty, and so forth—had been considered outside the proper sphere of business competence. Ideological change resulted in new standards and an expanded sphere of competence. This change in ideology entailed a change in activity, and without understanding the former we cannot explain the latter.

Although "conscious design" played a part in its formation, corporate social policy is at the same time an example of "symbolic politics" in the sense that its principal consequence is to establish the legitimacy of the profit-seeking corporation, to promote public "quiescence" rather than solve society's problems.[16] This consequence may be intended or unintended. Establishing legitimacy is an intended effect of Bank of America's social policy. Leland Prussia, the chairman, conscious of the dangerous world in which the corporation operates, lists the threats that a failure to establish legitimacy may hold for an international bank.

> No matter how well an international bank performs on a global scale, if it fails to listen actively and respond visibly to the social needs prevalent in individual markets, it can become a broad target for strangling legislation, regulation, nationalization, or even for violent mob or terrorist attacks. All multinational corporations, and banks in particular, must reinforce the public perception that business is serving society's needs.[17]

It is not being suggested that the symbolic nature of corporate social policy constitutes deception. In putting the case for social policy,

16. See Murray Edelman, *The Symbolic Uses of Politics* (Urbana: University of Illinois Press, 1964), p. 172.

17. Paper presented to the annual Institute of Bankers Cambridge Seminar, Cambridge, England, September 15, 1981.

many businessmen openly argue that business faces legitimacy problems. And critics of corporate social responsibility from both the right and the left have testified to the sincerity and dedication of business social policy-makers, for some of whom legitimacy may be a secondary consideration to fulfilling what they perceive as their social responsibilities.[18]

There are, however, limits to corporate social responsibility.[19] The ideology that shapes corporate social policy continues to recognize the importance of profit at the same time as it promotes non-profit-generating activities, and the corporation operates within a framework of constraints that prevent substantial and prolonged deviation from profit. So, for example, in those times when corporate social policy is most needed—during economic recession and depression—its subordinate relation to profit is likely to make it most scarce. In brief, the origin and development of corporate social policy is inextricably linked to questions of legitimacy and it is likely to be more successful in addressing them than in responding to society's problems. In his novel *Jailbird*, Kurt Vonnegut tells of a situation in which social policy strayed too far from its symbolic role.

> So we ordered more beers. Uncle Alex would later become a cofounder of the Indianapolis chapter of Alcoholics Anonymous, although his wife would say often and pointedly that he himself had never been an alcoholic. He began to talk now about The Columbia Conserve Company, a cannery that Powers Hapgood's father, William, also a Harvard man, had founded in Indianapolis in 1903. It was a famous experiment in industrial democracy, but I had never heard of it before. There was a lot that I had never heard of before.

18. See Robert Heilbroner, "The View from the Top: Reflections on a Changing Business Ideology," in Earl F. Cheit, ed., *The Business Establishment* (New York: Wiley and Sons, 1964), p. 21.

19. See Neil W. Chamberlain, *The Limits of Corporate Responsibility* (New York: Basic Books, 1973) for a discussion of economic constraints on corporate social policy.

The Columbia Conserve Company made tomato soup
and chili and catsup, and some other things. It was mas-
sively dependent on tomatoes. The company did not make
a profit until 1916. As soon as it made one, though, Powers Hapgood's father began to give his employees some of
the benefits he thought workers everywhere in the world
were naturally entitled to. The other principal stockholders were his two brothers, also Harvard men—and they
agreed with him.

So he set up a council of seven workers, who were to
recommend to the board of directors what the wages and
working conditions should be. The board, without any
prodding from anybody, had already declared that there
would no longer be any seasonal lay-offs, even in such a
seasonal industry, and that there would be vacations with
pay, and that medical care for workers and their dependents would be free, and that there would be sick pay and
a retirement plan, and that the ultimate goal of the company was that, through a stock-bonus plan, it become the
property of the workers.

"It went bust," said Uncle Alex, with a certain grim,
Darwinian satisfaction.[20]

Businessmen have never been satisfied with attributing their activity solely to self-interest. Historically, an assortment of justifications have been adduced for capitalism, beginning with the legality
of selfishness, based on property rights arguments. An early version
is John Locke's interpretation, in the *Second Treatise*, of property
rights derived from natural law in a way consistent with capitalist
economic arrangements.[21] Such arguments are still asserted today.
A second justification is the divinity of selfishness, derived from
Protestantism and described by Max Weber. A third type is the
science of selfishness based on classical economics and later on
Herbert Spencer's misapplication of Darwinian theory; this is as-

20. *Jailbird* (New York: Dell, 1979), p. 16.

21. See Neil J. Mitchell, "John Locke and the Rise of Capitalism," *History of
Political Economy* 18, no. 2 (1986).

sociated with nineteenth-century capitalism. A fourth justification is the denial or deferral of selfishness, based on the claim of social responsibility that characterizes twentieth-century American capitalism. The familiar argument that democracy is at least sometimes a by-product of capitalism is one of several subsidiary justifications.

Failure to establish legitimacy jeopardizes power; it may prompt legislation and regulation, and even endanger the corporation's survival. But to describe corporate social policy as linked in this way to long-run profit maximization begs the question of why it has become necessary for corporations to behave in this manner. After all, even the advertising benefits of corporate social policies are indirect, since an institution rather than a product is being advertised. Posing the problem as one of legitimacy, rather than, say, advertising, directs analytic attention to institutional power, threats to power, and the ways in which ideology and policy help maintain that power. Without reducing social policies to an aspect of profit seeking, this approach shows how a variety of issues—social policy activity, its association with large firms, the change in businessmen's belief system, public attitudes, and state activity towards business—are related to the corporation's dominant goal: profit.

In viewing the corporation as a political institution, it is important to stress that the process of legitimation does not operate in a mechanistic way. Of course, it is possible for individual decision makers, living dangerously, to turn a deaf ear—or a strong arm, for that matter—towards questions about the legitimacy of their power. People in political life have alternatives. The attempt here is to specify the conditions under which corporate social policy-making is likely. Thus, large, undepressed firms controlled by decision makers who subscribe to the ideology of social responsibility—especially those who have recently weathered hostile public criticism and consequently are worried about government interference—are most likely to make social policy. Yet this explanation and the alternatives described in chapters 3 and 4 are not mutually exclusive. It might be expected that officials of management-controlled corporations would feel legitimacy demands more intensely, and rely more heavily on claims of corporate social responsibility, than officials of owner-controlled corporations, who can still avail themselves of the property rights argument. So far, however, there is little empirical support for this expectation. Unions fit most easily into this explanation as one of the groups that can contribute to corporate legitimacy problems by raising questions about the exercise of corporate power, but that on their own pose an insufficient threat to account for the wide range of corporate social policies.

Such is the case for viewing the corporation as a political institution. It remains to apply this perspective to American business experience in the first three decades of this century, the period in which the nineteenth-century ideology and the science of selfishness were replaced by an ideology of business power and the denial of selfishness.

six

Remaking the American Capitalist Class I: Nineteenth-Century Ideology

Since Lenin's *What Is to Be Done?*, working-class consciousness has been a focus of considerable intellectual and political attention. It is recognized as a critical element in the economic and political choices of members of the working class, and even as constitutive of the term *class*. Marxists work and wait for the leap from "trade-union consciousness" to "revolutionary consciousness," while non-Marxists may point to the durability of traditional political beliefs and particularly to the continuing importance of nationalism. But both agree on the significance of working-class consciousness for the prospects of economic, social, and political change. In this chapter I will discuss capitalist class consciousness or ideology, which is also presumed to be of significance for institutions and relationships in industrial society. Social and economic stability, not change, is the measure of its success.

The turn of the century in America was a transitional ideological period when the nineteenth-century science of selfishness was discarded in favor of a new ideology that acknowledged business power and proclaimed social responsibility. In the old ideology, the pursuit of profit and private accumulation of property were linked with social advancement. The idea that the present and future well-being of the community as a whole was ineluctably bound to private selfishness became a theoretical proposition of economics with Adam Smith, a biological imperative with Herbert Spencer, and an economic dogma with Milton Friedman. It is argued that mankind will benefit most if labor and goods become commodities in a perfectly competitive and therefore self-regulating market, subject to an inviolable, freely fluctuating price mechanism. The new ideology, by contrast, charges businessmen with duties other than profit maximization. To the narrow concern with profit is added a notion of social responsibility, which presupposes power rather than subjugation to market forces. The public good becomes an intended rather than an unintended objective, placing businessmen on the uncertain ground of defining this objective, rather than relying on the apparently neutral, impersonal, and uncontrollable market system to establish public priorities.

Between the 1890s and the 1920s a change took place in the aims and rules of conduct of large firms, the most important section of the American business community. The new rules expanded the corporation's sphere of action to social as well as economic matters. Two major shifts in orientation characterized this ideological transformation: first, a shift from private, openly selfish activities toward public, apparently unselfish ones; and second, a shift from quietism to social activism on the part of businesses. This chapter describes the content of nineteenth-century business ideology. The next chapter will discuss its inadequacies in the face of industrial and social change and the factors that led to the development of a new ideology. Chapter 8 deals with this new ideology, focusing on its social policy implications.

For a policy choice to be defensible, it must be shown at minimum that it is within the institution's proper sphere of action, that the choice represents a proper use of resources, and that the policy is fair. As Charles Anderson has demonstrated, whether a policy choice satisfies the standards of authority, efficiency, and equity depends "on the ideological, disciplinary, or cultural context within which we are operating."[1] In the nineteenth century a business ideology based on classical economic theory and the fundamental unity of private and public interest provided the context for policy choices and Anderson's "logic of evaluation."

1. "The Place of Principles in Policy Analysis," *The American Political Science Review* 73 (September 1979), p. 714.

From the Civil War to the turn of the century, the classical economic doctrine of laissez-faire "was championed in America as it
never was before and has never been since." Among Americans,
Jean-Baptiste Say's *Treatise on Political Economy,* Harriet Marti-
neau's *Illustrations of Political Economy,* and Francis Wayland's *Elements of Political Economy* were particularly popular texts.[2] Marti-
neau's nine volumes introduced the layman to the principles of
classical economic theory through illustrative narratives. Wayland,
too, aimed at widespread dissemination; in his words, the book
was "serviceable either to the general student, or to the practical
merchant."[3]

The methodological perspective underlying classical economics
is that the study of economics is fundamentally similar to that of
the natural sciences. The recurring patterns of economic events are
describable in a few general laws or principles. Social scientists can
observe these laws, but they cannot modify them through policy.
The modern critique of the scientific approach to social life centers
on the proposition that social phenomena differ fundamentally
from natural phenomena in that man's activity is goal-directed and
intentional. Thus, specific cultural factors influence the formation
of goals and the constituents of intentions. This being the case, it
is impossible to formulate a small number of general laws without
adding many complicating reservations and qualifications. In this
view, the idea of constant conjunction that is the essence of the
attribution of causality in the natural sciences is confounded by
man's ability to choose among alternatives.[4] This critique is neatly
preempted in classical economic theory by conceding intentional
activity but assuming only one intention. Human activity becomes
predictable, or reducible to general laws, when the single aim of
commercial gain is assumed.

2. Sidney Fine, *Laissez Faire and the General Welfare State: A Study of Conflict in American Thought, 1865–1901* (Ann Arbor: University of Michigan Press,
1956), p. 29 and pp. 10–11.

3. *Elements of Political Economy* (Austin: Gould and Lincoln, 1853), p. iii.

4. See Alasdair MacIntyre, "A Mistake about Causality in Social Science,"
in Peter Laslett and W. G. Runciman, eds., *Philosophy, Politics and Society,* 2d
Series (Oxford: Blackwell, 1962).

According to classical economic theory, this aim unintentionally serves the public interest. Public and private interest coincide when economic activity takes place in the competitive market. If numerous buyers and sellers in each industry possess a knowledge of each others' activities, then no single buyer or seller can influence price. Competition creates continuous pressure to produce at the lowest possible costs and at the same time prevents more than temporary excess profits. Thus, an efficient allocation of economic resources is assured. Not only is it impossible for an individual to directly affect the public good or general welfare, it is unnecessary.

While it is Adam Smith's image of an "invisible hand" that endures, versions of this doctrine of a harmony of private and public interest have been unearthed in the works of earlier French as well as English writers. Montaigne advanced the notion that private vices, often defined in terms of lust or ambition instead of commercial gain, may have virtuous results. Antoine de Montchrétien, an early seventeenth-century French dramatist, argued on the same lines, including in his view a place for the state to encourage productivity, discourage idleness, and unfetter internal trade, among other things.[5] But Smith's most famous forerunner was Bernard Mandeville, who wrote in the "Fable of the Bees": "Thus every part was full of vice, / Yet the whole mass a paradise." However, he, too, relied on "the Dextrous Politician" to resolve the paradox of "private vices" and "publick benefits."[6] Smith, as Elie Halevy points out, transposed private "vices" into private "interests."

> But what is it that Mandeville calls evil or vice? Is it egoism? If egoism is useful to the public, and if further it be agreed to call virtuous such qualities in individuals as are useful to the public, why persist in calling egoism a vice? This is the criticism which was brought against Mandeville by all the moralists connected with the utili-

5. See Nannerl Keohane, *Philosophy and the State in France* (Princeton: Princeton University Press, 1980), pp. 165–66.

6. Albert O. Hirschman, *The Passions and the Interests: Political Arguments for Capitalism before its Triumph* (Princeton: Princeton University Press, 1977), p. 18.

tarian tradition, from Hume and Brown down to Godwin
and Malthus. If Mandeville had started by reconsidering
the current terminology, which was founded on the notions of an erroneous and confused morality, he would
have discovered the thesis of the identity of interests and
would have worked to advance moral science instead of
acting the litterateur and maker of paradoxes. For political
economy, ever since Adam Smith, has rested entirely on
the thesis of the natural identity of interests.[7]

Smith also severely restricted the role of the state, arguing that
external interference with the market would disturb its natural efficiency. "Laissez-faire" was the state's guiding principle. Unable
to make a positive contribution to economic welfare, it should be
no more active than was necessary to preserve the inequalities
created by private property. "It is only under the shelter of the civil
magistrate that the owner of that valuable property . . . can sleep a
single night in security . . . Where there is no property . . . civil
government is not necessary."[8] Smith thus arrives at Locke's central
conclusion in the *Second Treatise*, though with none of the latter's
ambiguity in defining property.

Under Smith's system, the market controlled the demand for and
supply of labor. An increase in the demand for labor would increase
its price and so increase the supply by encouraging the "marriage
and multiplication of labourers." If supply exceeded demand, the
price for labor would fall. "It is in this manner that the demand for
men, like that of any other commodity, necessarily regulates the
production of men."[9] Defining men as commodities excluded the
possibility of a nonexploitative or human relationship between employer and employee. Wages were depressed to the necessaries of
survival and sometimes lower. In classical economic theory, the
equilibrium price of labor becomes, as David Ricardo put it, "that
price which is necessary to enable the labourers, one with another,

7. *The Growth of Philosophic Radicalism* (Boston: Beacon Press, 1966),
p. 15.
8. *The Wealth of Nations*, vol. 2, p. 232.
9. Ibid., vol. 1, p. 89.

to subsist and to perpetuate their race, without either increase or diminution."[10] High wages will encourage population increase, population increase will make labor plentiful, and thus the price of labor will fall.

It is the name of Thomas Malthus that is most closely associated with this dynamic. It was he who described it in its starkest terms and drew out its explicit policy implications. Malthus's basic premises are that "food is necessary to the existence of man" and that "the passion between the sexes is necessary and will remain nearly in its present state." Population increases geometrically, while subsistence increases only arithmetically.

> The power of population is so superior to the power in
> the earth to produce subsistence for man, that premature
> death must in some shape or other visit the human race.
> The vices of mankind are active and able ministers of de-
> population. They are the precursors in the great army of
> destruction; and often finish the dreadful work them-
> selves. But should they fail in this war of extermination,
> sickly seasons, epidemics, pestilence, and plague, advance
> in terrific array, and sweep of their thousands and tens of
> thousands. Should success be still incomplete, gigantic
> inevitable famine stalks in the rear, and with one mighty
> blow, levels the population with the food of the world.[11]

Clearly this is not a reformer's vision. According to Malthus, efforts to interfere with this grisly process only made it worse. He argued that England's poor laws actually worsened social conditions by increasing population without contributing to any increase in the means of subsistence, and thus reducing the quantity that the labor of those in work would purchase. They, too, would end up seeking assistance. The operation of economic principles was for observing,

10. *On the Principles of Political Economy and Taxation* (1817; reprint, Harmondsworth, Middlesex: Penguin, 1971), p. 115.

11. *An Essay on the Principle of Population* (1798; reprint, New York: Random House, 1960), pp. 51–52.

not modifying. "To prevent the recurrence of misery, is, alas! beyond the power of man."[12]

These, then, are the theoretical propositions on which nineteenth-century business ideology drew. Economic activity in the
market was self-correcting, an efficient use of resources, and should
be left undisturbed by political institutions. This line of reasoning
had an obvious appeal to businessmen, who were instructed to seek
only their own gain, secure in the knowledge that in doing so they
benefited society. Even if they were to permit themselves a charitable impulse, it could do little good and was more likely to do
harm. In addition, classical economic theory's status as a science
removed it from moral criticism. The president of the Chicago, Burlington, and Quincy Railroad said in 1884, "If I were able I would
found a school for the study of political economy in order to harden
men's hearts."[13] According to an article in the *American Journal of
Sociology* in 1896, "a very common conviction of employers" was
expressed by a manufacturer's comment that the "relation between
capital and labor is one of the many questions in the comprehensive
science of political economy, and as such is a purely business matter. Philanthropy has nothing to do with it, nor has religion or
sentiment, any more than they have to do with astronomy or with
the law of gravitation."[14] H. O. Havemeyer, president of the Sugar
Trust and forthright espouser of the ideology, remarked in 1900 that
"business is not a philanthropy . . . I do not care two cents for your
ethics. I do not know how to apply them."[15] From this ideological
perspective, if discontent arises with poverty or unemployment, the
problem for those in authority is not to provide more food or work
but to properly communicate the explanation of these "natural conditions." Karl Marx, in a discussion of the "mental vacuity of the
English bourgeoisie," provides a nice example of this type of analysis. "Thus Dr. Kay, for example, in his pamphlet *Recent Measures*

12. Ibid., p. 38.

13. Fine, *Laissez Faire*, p. 101.

14. C. R. Henderson, "Business Men and Social Theorists," *The American
Journal of Sociology* 2 (January 1896), p. 387.

15. Joseph Dorfman, *Thorstein Veblen and His America* (New York: Viking,
1934), pp. 150–51.

for the Promotion of Education in England, reduces everything to neglected education. Guess why! Owing to lack of education, the worker does not understand the 'natural laws of trade,' laws which necessarily reduce him to pauperism. That is why he rebels."[16]

Although the tendency towards industrial concentration was plain by the last decade of the nineteenth century, businessmen and their apologists continued to assert the validity of principles developed in the context of a decentralized economy—a good illustration of the sway of defunct economists on practical men. In an article entitled "Facts about Trusts," Charles F. Beach, Jr., argued that while trusts were a "natural evolution" in business, sustained excess profits were impossible "without tempting the cupidity of men in other lines and creating at once an outside competition."[17] Henry Wood, in "The Bugbear of Trusts," gave his readers a similar assurance. He likened excess profits to a weight that could be lifted artificially, so defying the law of gravity, and asserted that the "economic no less than the physical law remains operative . . . and, sooner or later, the artificial obstructions are overcome."[18]

The enthusiastic reception accorded classical economics in America turned to rapture when Herbert Spencer added a biological twist. On this there is rare agreement among historians. Spencer was "honored in the United States as no philosopher ever was in Greece, no artist in Renaissance Italy, no scientist anywhere in his own day," and social Darwinism won America "as no philosophy had ever won a nation before."[19] Another historian writes that "no visiting philosopher before or since has received such a reception as was accorded Spencer in his triumphant visit to America in 1882."[20] Spencer was without honor only in his own country. In a letter to Andrew Carnegie he expressed his chagrin, saying that his

16. "Critical Notes on Social Reform," in William Connolly, ed., *Legitimacy and the State* (Oxford: Blackwell, 1984), p. 23.

17. *Forum* 8 (September 1889), p. 68.

18. *Forum* 5 (July 1888), p. 586.

19. Thomas C. Cochran and William Miller, *The Age of Enterprise* (New York: Macmillan, 1960), pp. 119–20.

20. Alan P. Grimes, *American Political Thought* (New York: Holt, 1955), p. 302. See also Fine, *Laissez Faire,* p. 32.

work had been "hindered by the English public." The *Spectator*, he said, "disposed of *First Principles* in a score of lines of small type among its notices of third rate or ephemeral works." He noted that for thirty-four years the *Edinburgh Review* "wholly ignored" him and then, to add insult to injury, "gave currency to a contemptuous article on *First Principles* by Lord Grimthorpe."[21]

To what, then, did Spencer owe his popularity in the United States? Historians agree that in an "age of enterprise," his work put contemporary American business practice in the context of a progressive evolution. "To a generation singularly engrossed in the competitive pursuit of industrial wealth, it gave cosmic sanction to free competition."[22] Sidney Fine notes that "his application to society of Darwin's theory suited the tastes of the American businessman."[23] Richard Hofstadter writes:

> How, then, can one account for the ascendency, until the 1890s, of the rugged individualist's interpretation of Darwinism? The answer is that American society saw its own image in the tooth-and-claw version of natural selection, and that its dominant groups were therefore able to dramatize this vision of competition as a thing good in itself. Ruthless business rivalry and unprincipled politics seemed to be justified by the survival philosophy. As long as the dream of personal conquest and individual assertion motivated the middle class, this philosophy seemed tenable, and its critics remained a minority.[24]

What Charles Darwin saw in South American animal life, social Darwinists discovered in North American social life: from Darwin we have the descent of man, from Spencer the ascent of the businessman.

Darwin himself connected biology with economics when he de-

21. Burton J. Hendrick, *The Life of Andrew Carnegie* (New York: Doubleday, 1932), vol. 2, p. 286.

22. Cochran and Miller, *The Age of Enterprise*, p. 119.

23. *Laissez Faire*, p. 43.

24. *Social Darwinism in American Thought* (Boston: Beacon Press, 1955), p. 201.

scribed his theory as "the doctrine of Malthus applied with manifold force to the whole animal and vegetable kingdoms, for in this case there is no artificial increase of food, and no prudential restraint from marriage."[25] The social Darwinists returned Malthus, in reconstituted form, to economics in their extremist rendering of nineteenth-century business ideology. The transposition of Darwin's theory to human society reinforced the central tenets of classical economic theory—self-interest equals public interest, competition, and laissez-faire—by implanting them with new significance. The progress and development of the social organism now depended on adherence to these tenets. Darwin consciously avoided attributing to his theory of "descent with modification" any suggestion that the process signified progress; he eschewed the term *evolution* partly because it might carry this connotation. Nevertheless, many of his readers drew evaluative conclusions, and the ideological power of social Darwinism rested on this distortion.[26]

Human life for social Darwinists was a competitive struggle for survival in which the fittest survived, while the weak, and their character traits, perished. This natural process, if left to itself, resulted in social improvement. Domestically, the future belonged to captains of industry, internationally to white Western nations. Social Darwinism justified oppressive colonial relationships and, in the domestic economy, the presence of both great wealth and great poverty. In the economic struggle for existence, money was a precise measure of fitness, with millionaires and their host institutional structures demonstrating that they were the fittest. James J. Hill, a railroad owner, claimed that "the fortunes of the railroad companies are determined by the law of the survival of the fittest."[27] Arguing in *Forum* that increasing social differentiation was essential to social development, Frederick Hawley claimed that "the highest social functions can be adequately performed only by the favorites of fortune."[28] Social inequalities, according to the social Darwinists,

25. *The Origin of Species* (1859; reprint, New York: Mentor, 1958), p. 75.

26. Stephen J. Gould, *Ever Since Darwin: Reflections on Natural History* (New York: W. W. Norton, 1979), pp. 36–38.

27. Hofstadter, *Social Darwinism*, p. 45.

28. "Edward Atkinson's Economic Theories," *Forum* 7 (May 1889), p. 304.

were natural, eternal, and beyond human control. "The inequalities of society are largely the result of natural forces, which is another way of saying that there will always be many grades of prosperity and adversity," wrote Henry D. Chapin.[29]

What particularly recommended social Darwinism was that in it a place could be found for corporate trusts or industrial concentration. John D. Rockefeller, Jr., is reported to have said in one of his Sunday school addresses that "large business is merely a survival of the fittest. The American Beauty rose can be produced in the splendor and fragrance which bring cheer to its beholder only by sacrificing the early buds which grow up around it. This is not an evil tendency in business. It is merely the working out of a law of nature and a law of God."[30] The evolution of large corporations was a natural result of the competitive struggle for existence. They had survived; therefore they had proved their fitness to survive. The ideological advance over classical theory was that for the public interest to be served, it was no longer necessary for self-interest to work in a perfectly competitive market; public interest was now defined in broader terms than the most economically efficient allocation of resources, incorporating the less tangible notions of racial and social progress. Moreover, the competition could be won under social Darwinism, thus providing a place for trusts, whereas winning in classical economic theory was always transitory and ultimately self-defeating, for the victors always ended up with new competitors.

The linguistic symbolism of social Darwinism created the perception of the successful businessman as the height of virility, the hope of the age, and at the same time deflected criticism by consigning the businessman's critics—those who wanted to rearrange the economic structure—to a futile, antiscientific camp. The policy implications of these ideas were clear. Inaction was prescribed. Neither businessmen nor the state could or should consciously attempt to improve the social situation. Inequality and poverty were not

29. "Preventable Causes of Poverty," *Forum* 7 (June 1889), p. 417.

30. William J. Ghent, *Our Benevolent Feudalism* (New York: Macmillan, 1902), p. 29.

social problems to be addressed by policy, but instead were defined as part of the natural order—that is, as conditions out of the reach of policy makers. In fact, social Darwinist reasoning attributed positive and progressive results to these conditions. The only hope dangled in front of the poor was the possibility that certain individuals might overcome their situation through self-help. "The indigent poor classes are those who lack intelligence, skill, industry, economy, and self control," wrote W. T. Harris.[31] Poverty was a moral as well as an economic category. "The first essential act in the effort to aid the struggle for subsistence among the poor, must be to try and dissipate some of the gross ignorance and shiftlessness that so often accompany it."[32] Thus it was that Andrew Carnegie built 2,507 buildings for public libraries.

The most uncompromising of social Darwinists was a Yale professor of political science, William Graham Sumner. In his work, all the elements of the creed are set out with ruthless clarity. Large fortunes, he tells us, are "not at all a thing to be regretted" but a "necessary condition of many forms of social advance."[33] Class distinctions merely reflect the ability of men to make the most of their opportunities. Any attempt to change things is pointless, for "God and Nature have ordained the chances and conditions of life on earth once for all."[34] Poverty and misery are the natural penalties for poor performance in the struggle. Social reform transfers the penalty "from the head of the man who has incurred it to heads of others who have not incurred it." And so, for Sumner, a "drunkard in the gutter is just where he ought to be, according to the fitness and tendency of things."[35] Within his social and economic system there are only two tasks for government—"the property of men and the honor of women. These it has to defend against crimes."[36] He sees the specific relationship between employers and employees as

31. "Edward Bellamy's Vision," *Forum* 8 (October 1889), p. 201.
32. Chapin, "Preventable Causes of Poverty," p. 418.
33. *What Social Classes Owe to Each Other* (New York: Harper and Bros., 1883), p. 54.
34. Ibid., p. 14.
35. Ibid., p. 131.
36. Ibid., p. 101.

determined by contract according to the rules of the market. To regard employers and employees as partners, he argues, "is a delusive figure of speech."[37] He goes so far as to argue that "industrial war" is a healthy economic sign, important to the maintenance of liberty, a legitimate resort in the bargaining process, and a method of reallocating capital and labor. Sumner advanced this argument in the era of the Homestead strike, when "war" was a fair description of industrial relations. It was at Homestead that Alexander Berkman shot and wounded Henry Frick, chairman of the Carnegie Steel Company, in his office. The National Amalgamated Association of Iron and Steel Workers had called a strike in 1892. The company response was to hire three hundred Pinkertons and arm them with Winchester rifles. After bloodshed the strike was broken. Sumner declared: "Industrial war is a sign of vigor in society . . . It is not possible to stop it . . . and it will be wise philosophy and statesmanship not to try."[38] The appeal of such doctrines to corporations, who held the balance of power, is obvious.

Carnegie considered himself one of Spencer's disciples. His famous essay "The Gospel of Wealth," which appeared in 1889, was written in the language of social Darwinism and was generally faithful to its doctrines. The question Carnegie poses in his essay is, "What is the proper mode of administering wealth after the laws upon which civilization is founded have thrown it into the hands of the few?"[39] He argues that an individual's wealth should not be bequeathed, for that may harm the recipients, nor left at death for the public use, for that may become a "monument of his folly," but should be regarded as a "trust fund" for the community and given away by the businessman while he is still alive. Carnegie argued that in making his fortune the businessman must follow accepted business practices, but having made it, he then acquired wider social responsibilities. It was assumed that the businessman was a better judge of the proper use of wealth than government. Of course, Carnegie held strong views about worthwhile causes consistent

37. Ibid., p. 85.

38. "Do We Want Industrial Peace?" *Forum* 8 (December 1889), p. 416.

39. *The Gospel of Wealth and Other Timely Essays* (1887; reprint, Cambridge, Mass.: Harvard University Press, 1962), p. 16.

with the self-help doctrine, asserting "that the best means of benefiting the community is to place within its reach the ladders upon
which the aspiring can rise."[40] This argument, and the notion of the
businessman "conspiring knowingly for the public good" (to re-
phrase a line of Hirschman's), makes Carnegie a transitional figure
between nineteenth-century ideology and the new business ideology.

Under nineteenth-century business ideology, the goal of economic activity is restricted to profit. This restriction is self-
imposing in the sense that it coincides with man's psychological
characteristics and the demands of the economic system. The goal
of profit is consistent with a view of man as essentially selfish.
Since the method of economic activity is competition in the market,
to depart from this goal is in neither the firm's nor the public's
interest. External interference with competition upsets the efficient
allocation of resources. As a consequence, the state is viewed with
hostility. The components of economic activity, both capital and
labor, are represented as numerous and in themselves powerless.
Firms are subject to market forces and have no capacity for choice.
For the social Darwinists, who recognized the existence of trusts,
these monopolistic institutions represented a product of natural
evolution and were not subject to human control. At the same time,
some social Darwinists continued to assert the presence and "ultimate" decisiveness of competition. Andrew Carnegie said, "Trusts
cannot permanently thwart the laws of competition and hence must
prove beneficial agencies for the people."[41]

Labor is viewed as an individualized commodity under nineteenth-century business ideology. Labor's rights are a matter of individual contract between two equal and freely consenting parties.
This assertion is interesting to consider in relation to other aspects
of the ideology, particularly the economic and social importance of
physical necessity. "Hunger," William Townsend said, "will tame
the fiercest animals, it will teach decency and civility, obedience
and subjection to the most perverse. In general it is only hunger

40. Ibid., p. 28.
41. Ibid., p. 78.

which can spur and goad them [the poor] on to labour."[42] When the alternative to making the labor contract is starvation, government support having been ruled out, the notion of "consent" is emptied of its usual implication of the possession of alternatives. We end up with the Hobbesian understanding under which one's own death represents a real choice.

Under nineteenth-century ideology, the public interest is served indirectly by economic activity. Profit seeking with market guarantees of efficiency thus becomes its own justification. It is argued that this type of economic system contributes to individuality and freedom. "Private property and free competition constitute the simple device by which civilization has been able to isolate individuals from one another and develop a sense of the sacredness of personality."[43] In regard to social progress the ideology is quietist. Classical economic doctrine did not hold much hope for the possibility of improvement. For social Darwinists progress is slow, governed by laws beyond the influence of conscious action—organic as opposed to intentional change. Poverty, periodic unemployment, subsistence wages, and so on were necessary and even desirable conditions of the economic system and not social problems to be dealt with. Without them, what would prompt the shiftless to work? What would provide a testing ground in which the fittest could survive? In short, the firm is pictured as a purely profit seeking, powerless, and nonresponsible institution, operating in a competitive market, to be neither hindered nor helped by state activity. Thus, social policy is excluded under this ideology because it falls outside the authority of the firm and indeed of the state, represents an inefficient use of resources, and is unfair in transferring the penalty that should accompany failure onto successful firms.

This picture of the economic system distorted reality. In fact, corporations had power far in excess of individual workers, though they posed as equal contractors. The railways, while opposed to state interference, benefited from public land grants, and other in-

42. Quoted in Karl Polanyi, *The Great Transformation* (New York: Farrar and Rinehart, 1944), p. 113.
43. Harris, "Edward Bellamy's Vision," p. 207.

dustries benefited from protective tariffs. Tariffs were defended through the "infant" industry argument, but infancy could last a long time, like the "temporary" excess profits of corporations. The next chapter will examine the growth of discontent with this depiction of business roles and relationships and the factors that contributed to a crisis of corporate legitimacy.

seven

Remaking the American Capitalist Class II: Ideological Change at the Turn of the Century

American business ideology at the turn of the century embraced a crude notion that might makes right. The fittest survive, and should survive . . . This ideology did not meet its own first test—survival. How could it be sold to the majority of the electorate, since it was they who were billed as patsies in its scenario?

—Paul A. Samuelson

The process of ideological change occupies a critical place in social theory. In its various formulations, this process raises questions about the dynamics of social life that go to the heart of research in social science. This is the terrain on which Weber confronts Marx in accounting for the rise of capitalism. Marx labeled the alternative approaches "materialism" and "idealism." For him, economic structures determined ideology. Honor, chivalry, and loyalty perished with the collapse of feudal economic arrangements, as bourgeois individualism and nationalism would perish with the collapse of capitalism. The discovery of new markets, the surpassing of productive forces by demand, and the availability of new productive techniques produced capitalism. For Weber, it was not the tensions and strains of economic institutions and forces, but the motives of men that counted. When business came to be conas a vocation and profit as a religious obligation, then capitalism took off. It took off in Protestant England, not Catholic Italy.

The clash between Marx and Weber is a convenient way of situating the methodological poles, though it is debatable how pure a materialist Marx was. As is often the case, a middle position, while less than bold, is more defensible than an extreme one in interpreting the relationship of ideas to economic, political and social structures. An analysis of ideological change in early twentieth-century America suggests that the relationship between ideology and these structures should be viewed interactively. Changes in the American economy produced tension between new industrial structures and the old ideology, creating problems of legitimacy and the conditions for ideological change. This tension increased with the assertion of an ideology and its policy derivatives, rooted in an earlier economic era, that were now out of phase with their economic surroundings. The consequences of this ideological change were reflected in the development of corporate social policy, which facilitated the accommodation of the modern corporation to American society.

The analytical perspective of the corporation as a political institution, possessing power but also facing problems of legitimacy, thus directs attention to legitimacy problems in accounting for the process of ideological change. This perspective suggests the relevance of external as well as internal psychological and institutional factors. *The American Business Creed*, by Francis X. Sutton, Seymour E. Harris, Carl Kaysen, and James Tobin, offers a psychological explanation of business ideology. The contents of business ideology, the authors argue, can be explained in terms of the "psychological strains" under which businessmen operate. Ideology serves to reconcile the variety of roles a businessman has to perform as a businessman and as a member of society. "For the individual businessman, the function of ideology is to help him maintain his psychological ability to meet the demands of his occupation."[1] Reinhard Bendix, who examined American business ideology in the 1920s

1. *The American Business Creed* (Cambridge, Mass.: Harvard University Press, 1956), p. 11.

and the shift away from social Darwinism, suggests that the internal authority structure of the business institution is decisive in ideological change: "The changing images of American managerial ideology have reflected the increasing bureaucratization of economic enterprises."[2] Neglected in these accounts are the external influences directed at business as an institution, influences that shape the process of ideological change and explain the contents of ideology. They depoliticize the issue.

The political history of the rise of the modern corporation closely follows its economic history. Questions about the power of business—particularly the railroads—arose among the farming community. Gradually they broadened to include other social groups and industries as the nineteenth century drew to a close and industrial power became more concentrated. The railroads, by the nature of their task, were the first large firms. They induced mass production by expanding markets. The limited liability corporation provided the means to raise the necessary capital, while restricting the risk for stockholders solely to the capital invested. There were various methods of overcoming decentralization and competitiveness within an industry: informal agreements to pool production, cartels, trusts, holding companies, and mergers. An additional legal device that facilitated industrial concentration and monopoly was the patent. AT&T, for example, bought the patent rights on which its monopoly rested. Patent pooling agreements were organized to reduce conflict among large corporations and make entry into the industry by new competitors difficult.[3]

Standard Oil, the first great trust, was created in 1879, but it was not until after the mid-1890s that merger and concentration really took off. By 1904, two-fifths of manufacturing capital was owned by large combinations. Samuel Hays argues that the timing of this merger movement reflected the successful examples that Standard Oil and the American Tobacco Company had provided during the depression of the early 1890s, and the desire to take

2. *Work and Authority in Industry* (New York: Harper and Row, 1963), p. 319.

3. See David Noble, *America by Design* (New York: Alfred A. Knopf, 1977), p. 10.

advantage of a business boom during the latter part of the decade.[4] This turn-of-the-century wave of consolidation made nineteenth-century business ideology increasingly obsolete and undercut the assertion that a competitive market negated business power. The Progressive movement grew out of the popular realization that the competitive market was being destroyed.

It is easier to describe the economic history of the corporation than its political history. No opinion poll data are available to enable us to assess corporate legitimacy problems. But it is still possible to trace the salience of the corporation as a political issue: the more it becomes a political issue, the more it is seen to have legitimacy problems. Two means of examining the process by which the corporation became a political issue—that is, the failure of nineteenth-century ideology to make corporations acceptable—are analyses of party platforms and public policy towards corporations over a period of time. Parties can ignore or play down significant issues in their platforms, but they cannot do so over the long term without losing support. Thus, platforms represent an indirect "barometer of opinion" in American political history.[5] Despite the skepticism with which platforms and politicians' sincerity are often received, as Edward Tufte has said, "the arguments and priorities advanced by party platforms are often the very same arguments and priorities that are found at the heart of high-level economic policy making."[6]

In the 1872 election, both Democrats and Republicans condemned further grants of land to railroads. The Granger revolt, a popular movement of Midwestern and Western farmers and small businessmen against the railroads, had drawn attention to this issue. As monopolies, the railroads were perceived to be charging high rates while benefiting from public land grants and the appropriation of private land with government assistance. In 1876 the

4. *The Response to Industrialism, 1885–1914* (Chicago: University of Chicago Press, 1957), p. 50.

5. These and subsequent extracts from party platforms are taken from Kirk H. Porter and Donald B. Johnson, *National Party Platforms, 1840–1956* (Urbana: University of Illinois Press, 1956), p. vii.

6. *Political Control of the Economy* (Princeton: Princeton University Press, 1978), p. 76.

Democratic party platform called for the cessation of public land grants to railroads, claiming that the Republicans had already "squandered two hundred millions of acres" in this way. The Republicans, meanwhile, reaffirmed their opposition "to further grants of the public lands to corporations and monopolies," as they were to do in 1880. The Democratic position remained the same in 1880, with a statement about restricting public land to settlers' use. The small Greenback party, dedicated to an expansion of the money supply, was the most hostile to corporations. It called for, among other things, factory inspections, a federal bureau of labor statistics, and federal regulation of railroad rates, and denounced the two major parties for fostering monopolies. But this was a minority position. The year 1880 saw the election of a Republican president, James A. Garfield, a social Darwinist. While noting that "poverty is uncomfortable," he argued that "nine times of ten the best thing that can happen to a young man is to be tossed overboard and compelled to sink or swim for himself. In all my acquaintance I never knew a man to be drowned who was worth the saving."[7]

While the Democrats reiterated their earlier position, as well as demanding an end to "corporate abuses," the Republicans proposed public regulation of railroad rates in 1884. The Greenbacks again condemned "gigantic corporate monopolies" and the Anti-Monopoly party, which nominated the same candidates as the Greenbacks, devoted its platform to condemning corporate practices. Although Grover Cleveland was elected—the first Democratic president in almost thirty years—a change of party did not signify a fundamental change in ideas. In vetoing a bill that would have distributed seeds to drought-hit Texas, Cleveland said "that the lesson should be enforced that though the people support the Government the Government should not support the people."[8] The spoils system was Cleveland's major concern, although he advocated tariff reduction (principally as a means of reducing a treasury surplus) and estab-

7. Arthur M. Schlesinger, Jr., and Fred L. Israel, eds., *History of American Presidential Elections, 1789–1968* (New York: McGraw-Hill, 1971), vol. 2, p. 1,507.

8. Ibid., p. 1,616.

lished the Interstate Commerce Commission to oversee railroad rates.[9]

In the Democratic platform of 1888, criticism of corporations had a broader focus than the railroads and the tariff system was attacked as destructive of competition: "The interests of the people are betrayed, when, by unnecessary taxation, trusts and combinations are permitted and fostered, which, while unduly enriching the few that combine, rob the body of our citizens by depriving them of the benefits of natural competition."[10] The Democrats claimed to have retrieved almost one hundred million acres from corporations and returned it to the people. The Republicans criticized Democratic "free tradism," but the Republican platform declared its opposition "to all combinations of capital organized in trusts." Two labor parties ran candidates for the first time in 1888; both advocated government ownership of the means of communication and transportation. Benjamin Harrison, the Republican, won in 1888, to be beaten by Cleveland in 1892.

Giving a prominent place to the cause of tariff reform, the Democrats, in 1892, blamed the tariff for wage reductions, lack of general prosperity, and development of trusts "which are designed to enable capital to secure more than its just share of the joint product of Capital and Labor." The Republicans restated their belief in protectionism and were satisfied to endorse the Sherman Act of 1890. The Populist party in 1892 added to the general concern over corporations, stating that "the railroad corporations will either own the people or the people must own the railroads."[11] The Prohibition platform called for government control of railroad and telegraph industries and other "public corporations," and the Socialist Labor party advocated federal and municipal control of transportation, communication, and utility industries. Harrison blamed his defeat on the Homestead strike, economic problems, and working-class hostility to corporate wealth, though his personal unpopularity may have been an additional factor.[12]

9. Ibid., pp. 1,616–20
10. Porter and Johnson, *National Party Platforms*, p. 78.
11. Ibid., p. 91.
12. Schlesinger and Israel, *American Presidential Elections*, vol. 2, p. 1,731.

The 1890s saw the awakening of widespread public concern with corporate power. James Bryce observed of this decade that "all corporations are at present unpopular in America, and especially corporations possessed of monopolies." He claimed that railroad owners were behind only the president and the Speaker of the House in terms of the power they exercised. He noted at the same time that the politicians only held power "for four years and two years, while the railroad monarch may keep his for life."[13] In 1896, when William Jennings Bryan was the Democratic candidate for president, the party's platform proposed stricter federal controls on corporations to "protect the people from robbery and oppression." The Republican party emphasized the depressed economy and condemned the Democrats for not providing sufficient protection for U.S. industry. The National party, the People's party, and the Socialist Labor party all called for various forms of public ownership. Bryan lost the election by half a million votes.

From the last few years of the nineteenth century, when the wave of consolidation began, to 1912, the issue of corporate power dominated American politics. Concerns focused not only on economic matters like price fixing and discrimination, but on the political issue of corporate influence in legislative bodies. The Democrats pledged "unceasing warfare in nation, State and city against private monopoly in every form." Arguing that monopolies were the product of Republican policies, they called for removal of tariff protection for monopolies, more severe enforcement of antitrust laws, and laws to make corporate affairs public. One faction of the Populist, or People's, party described trusts as "the overshadowing evil of the age," and both factions demanded public ownership. The Prohibition platform of 1900, indicative of the importance of the corporation as a political issue, puts trusts and monopolies in the same category as demon drink. "The most dangerous [monopoly] of them all," it declared, was "the liquor power." The Social Democratic party and the Socialist Labor party defined themselves by their opposition to private corporations, and the other minor party in

13. *The American Commonwealth*, vol. 2 (New York: Macmillan, 1908), pp. 648–53.

1900, the Silver Republican party, condemned "combinations, trusts and monopolies." The Republican party platform preferred to focus attention on general economic prosperity and the American victory in the Spanish-American War. The platform did include a statement denouncing the creation of monopolies and pledged the party to correct abuses of monopolistic positions.

In 1904 the Democrats, to their electoral cost, fought a more conservative campaign, while Theodore Roosevelt "cut into the Democratic monopoly of championship of the underdog."[14] At the same time, the Socialists cut into Democratic support from the left. They still demanded an expansion of the power of the Interstate Commerce Commission, strict enforcement of civil and criminal laws against trusts and monopolies, and further legislation if necessary. They argued that large corporations exploited labor and that trusts and monopolies destroyed the free competition on which prosperity rested. Thus, elements of nineteenth-century business ideology were used as a basis for criticizing contemporary business practices, making this ideology an actual liability for corporations.

The People's party platform in 1904 declared that a "political democracy and an industrial despotism cannot exist side by side." Two Socialist parties fielded candidates in the election—a further indication of the political salience of corporate power. President Roosevelt was the Republican candidate. The party platform reflected Roosevelt's position that the advent of large corporations was part of an inevitable economic process, but that there were good and bad trusts. What was done with power, rather than power as such, was the issue for Republicans. The Republican platform stated: "Combinations of capital and of labor are the results of the economic movement of the age, but neither must be permitted to infringe upon the rights and interests of the people."[15] It is interesting that combinations of labor should have been mentioned, implying that corporations themselves might be victims of monopoly power, and that the traditional concept of the individually contract-

14. V. O. Key, Jr., *Politics, Parties, and Pressure Groups* (New York: Crowell, 1964), p. 175.
15. Porter and Johnson, *National Party Platforms*, p. 139.

ing employee was becoming outmoded. Roosevelt won the election by two and a half million votes over the Democrat, but the Socialist Eugene Debs got 402,895 votes—four times his total of 1900.

In 1908 Bryan was again the Democratic candidate, and again the most salient issue was the large corporation. The Democratic platform proposed federal licensing of corporations engaged in interstate commerce and legislation to prevent interlocking directorates. The new Independence party advocated public ownership of public utilities, as did the People's platform of 1908. The Republican platform began by reviewing the accomplishments of President Roosevelt, noting "first and foremost, a brave and impartial enforcement of the law, the prosecution of illegal trusts and monopolies."[16] With Roosevelt's blessing, William Howard Taft won the election. Debs, one of two Socialist candidates, added some 20,000 votes to his 1904 total.

The high noon of Progressivism, when corporate power was most conspicuous, was 1912. More than twelve hundred Socialists had been elected to public office in the preceding two years, and there were five daily Socialist newspapers.[17] The Democratic platform chastised Taft and the Republicans for failing to bring criminal charges against Standard Oil officials under the antitrust law. The Progressive party, true to Roosevelt's earlier position, recognized the large corporation as an inevitable outcome of economic development, but demanded federal regulation. "The existing concentration of vast wealth under a corporate system. . . . has placed in the hands of a few men enormous, secret, irresponsible power over the daily life of the citizen—a power insufferable in a free Government and certain of abuse."[18] Roosevelt's position went beyond the approach to the problem of the corporation embodied in the Sherman Act. While explicitly recognizing the power of the corporation, he substituted regulation and publicity of corporate activities for control through competition. The Democrat Woodrow Wilson won the 1912 election. The Progressive party, with more than four million

16. Ibid., p. 157.
17. Schlesinger and Israel, *American Presidential Elections*, vol. 2, p. 2,153.
18. Porter and Johnson, *National Party Platforms*, p. 178.

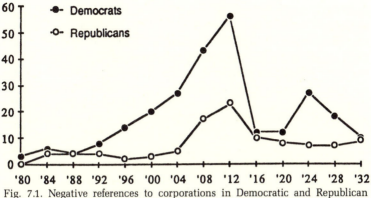

Fig. 7.1. Negative references to corporations in Democratic and Republican party platforms, 1880–1932

votes, came in second, the Republican party third, with three and a half million votes, and Debs got almost one million votes—the largest showing ever for a Socialist.

The increasing intensity of anticorporation sentiment and the growth of socialism as a minor political current in this period reflect the corporation's deepening legitimacy problems. The quantity of negative references to corporations in the major party platforms (fig. 7.1) represents a way of measuring the importance of the corporation as a political issue. References to corporate power in general and to individual industries and companies are included; references advocating regulation are taken as negative. The turning point is between 1896 and 1904, coinciding with the wave of consolidation. The issue of corporate power became increasingly salient up to 1912. Its diminishing importance as a political issue after that time can be attributed in part to its displacement by World War I, but it also reflects the success of the new ideology of business in legitimizing corporate power.

After the war the issue did not reemerge in its former strength, although it did not disappear. Senator Robert La Follette forced the Democrats to place more stress on the issue in 1924. He opened his platform by saying that the "great issue before the American people today is the control of government and industry by private monopoly" and won more than four million votes. Interestingly, the early years of the Great Depression were not used by political parties as an extraordinary opportunity to focus public attention on the issue of corporate power. It should be noted that even in America, where the major parties are traditionally considered more difficult to distinguish ideologically than are their European counterparts, there was a difference between the two major political parties on economic issues.[19] Both parties' platforms reflected the anticipated trend in the saliency of corporations as a political issue, but the Democrats were considerably more hostile to corporations than the Republicans. The precipitous dip in negative references by the Democrats in 1916 and 1920 may be an effect of their incumbency and their reluctance to criticize society or the economy, as well as the emergence of the war issue.

The recognition of corporate power as a political problem made it a target for public policy. Another way of monitoring the breakdown of nineteenth-century ideology and the development of corporate legitimacy problems is by tracing the formation of public policy in relation to the problem of corporate power. Antitrust policy reflected public officials' recognition of the illegitimacy of corporate power. In treating the development of antitrust policy as an indicator of a deepening legitimacy crisis for corporations, it should be understood that this policy actively modified corporate behavior. It constituted a threat to corporate independence, the exercise of corporate power, and even to corporate institutional survival. The problem for corporate officials was to remove the question of corporate power from the political agenda. They addressed this problem by reconceptualizing corporate social and economic relationships, transforming business ideology, and constructing corporate social policy.

From Thurman Arnold to Murray Edelman, antitrust policy has been seen as a prime example of "symbolic" politics. Arnold correctly observes that "the growth of great organizations in America occurred in the face of a religion which officially was dedicated to

19. In *Political Control of the Economy* (chapter 4), Tufte comes to a similar conclusion in his analysis of unemployment and inflation.

the preservation of the economic independence of individuals." While contrary to the principle of laissez-faire, the Sherman Act of 1890 reflected the importance that nineteenth-century ideology placed on competition in the proper functioning of the economic system. The act forbade "every contract, agreement, or combination in the form of a trust or otherwise in restraint of trade or commerce among the several states or with foreign nations." Arnold says that antitrust law was a "ceremony . . . which reconciled current mental pictures of what men thought society ought to be with reality."[20] Its function was no more than ceremonial because large corporations were an economic necessity. Edelman uses antitrust policy as an example of symbolic politics, of a state action that is largely empty of significant consequence, except to create a quiescent public. It is part of the "drama of state."[21]

Evaluated in terms of replacing concentration with competition, antitrust law cannot be judged a success. However, the Sherman Act and the antitrust legislation enacted by various states created great uncertainty for businessmen at the time. The possibility that antitrust law would shift from a ceremonial to a practical device encouraged changes in business thought and practice. Policy makers' use of antitrust law, together with judicial interpretation in the Progressive era, was intended to change business conduct, not to create a newly decentralized, competitive capitalism. Antitrust policy acquires new efficacy when considered from this perspective.

The language of the Sherman Act in condemning restraint of trade appeared clear, but the Supreme Court quickly introduced ambiguity. In a series of court cases, antitrust policy was made and remade. The first case to reach the Supreme Court under the act was the E. C. Knight case in 1895. The American Sugar Refining Company was charged with attempting to monopolize the production of sugar by acquiring four Philadelphia refineries, which gave the firm virtual control of refined sugar manufacturing in the United States. Chief Justice Melville Fuller argued that the power of Con-

20. *The Folklore of Capitalism* (New Haven: Yale University Press, 1937), p. 207.
21. *The Symbolic Uses of Politics*, p. 172.

gress extended only to interstate commerce; since the acquisition of the refineries concerned sugar manufacture in Pennsylvania, he refused to find the company in violation of the Sherman Act. This nonintervention was consistent with the dominant judicial philosophy of laissez-faire. The Knight case was the legal antecedent to the wave of consolidation that took place between 1897 and 1904.

In the same year as the Knight case, Eugene Debs and the American Railroad Union were taken to court under the Sherman Act. The union had organized the Pullman strike of 1894, and the Supreme Court ruled that it was in violation of antitrust law. The doctrine of laissez-faire, then, did not prohibit all government intervention in the economy. It was selective in that union activity could be controlled and protective tariffs and land grants to corporations were permitted. In other words, the government applied a laissez-faire policy whenever it benefited businessmen, but intervened when their power was threatened.

Congress, in response to the growing number of consolidations and the resulting public concern, established the United States Industrial Commission in 1898 to consider the problem and make recommendations. This commission proposed, among other things, federal licensing of corporations and the publication of annual reports by corporations. What emerged was the Bureau of Corporations, established in 1903, which had the power to investigate corporations and publish its findings.[22] By this time Roosevelt had come to dominate national politics. He saw himself as the popular champion of an autonomous state: "I am genuinely independent of the big monied men in all matters where I think the interests of the public are concerned, and probably I am the first President of recent times of whom this could be truthfully said."[23] By bringing antitrust proceedings against the Northern Securities Company in 1904, he made a public demonstration of the state's autonomy. In selecting Northern Securities, the administration confronted the most important individual capitalist of the era, John Pierpont Morgan. This

22. See James Weinstein, *The Corporate Ideal in the Liberal State, 1900–1918* (Boston: Beacon Press, 1968), p. 69.

23. Richard Hofstadter, *The Age of Reform* (New York: Alfred A. Knopf, 1959), p. 234.

action was the first since the Knight case to test the legality of the combination of competing companies before the Supreme Court.

Northern Securities was a New Jersey holding company established to bring under unified control the Northern Pacific and Great Northern railroads, as well as the Chicago, Burlington, and Quincy Railroad, which was jointly owned by the other two. These companies ran competing lines from the Great Lakes to the Pacific Ocean. U.S. Attorney General Philander C. Knox argued that "the device of a holding corporation for the purpose of circumventing the law can be no more effectual than any other means."[24] In reversing the direction it took in the Knight case and asserting the power of the federal government, the Supreme Court affirmed that "every corporation created by a State is necessarily subject to the supreme law of the land."[25] Prior to this case, it was widely believed that the holding company charter was exempt from the provisions of the Sherman Act. According to one commentator, "the trusts, which had enjoyed practical immunity for so long, were dumbfounded," and Morgan's response to prosecution was to rush to Washington to "fix it up."[26] He demanded to know whether Roosevelt was "going to attack [his] other interests." James J. Hill, president of the Great Northern Railway Company complained, "It really seems hard . . . that we should be compelled to fight for our lives against . . . political adventurers."[27]

The case represented a shift in doctrine away from "selective" laissez-faire, setting an ominous legal precedent for large corporations. The apparent reaffirmation of the market as the source of legitimacy and as the solution of the trust problem endangered institutions whose existence depended on overcoming market forces. The case demonstrated the essential unreliability of the old ideology as a legitimizer for large corporations. In the seven years following the Northern Securities decision, the National Industrial Conference Board found, "it was a commonly accepted view that

24. United States v. Northern Securities Co., 193 U.S. 301.

25. 193 U.S. 346.

26. Harold U. Faulkner, *The Quest for Social Justice, 1898–1914* (New York: Macmillan, 1931), p. 118.

27. Schlesinger and Israel, *American Presidential Elections*, vol. 3, p. 1,966.

every corporation, or even partnership, combining business units which had been previously competing, contravened the anti-trust law."[28] The Supreme Court's finding that one of Morgan's companies had violated the Sherman Act left lesser capitalists with little sense of security.

In understanding Roosevelt's antitrust policy and use of the Sherman Act, it is important to consider his views on large corporations and reform. In an address of 1902 entitled "Necessity of Establishing Federal Sovereignty over Trusts," he argued that "great corporations . . . are the creatures of the state" and the state has "the right to control them."[29] Significantly, Roosevelt did not question the corporation's existence; he conceived the problem as one of control. The proceeding against the Northern Securities Company did not spring from an indiscriminate support of competition, although it raised that possibility in businessmen's minds, not least because Knox argued that merely possessing the power to restrain trade constituted a violation of the law. Roosevelt, however, did not advocate dissolution but rather a distinction between "good" and "bad" trusts. (Actually, according to Amos Pinchot, this was Morgan's "pet distinction"; Roosevelt simply popularized it. It is ironic that his most famous victim was one of Morgan's companies.[30]) William Jennings Bryan had noted and scorned this distinction in accepting the Democratic presidential nomination in 1900. "Republicans who formerly abhorred a trust now beguile themselves with the delusion that there are good trusts and bad trusts."[31] In 1902 Roosevelt was saying, "We do not wish to destroy corporations, but we do wish to make them subserve the public good."[32] In 1906 he said, "It is unfortunate that our present laws should forbid all combinations, instead of sharply discriminating between those

28. *Mergers and the Law* (New York, 1929), p. 28.

29. *The Roosevelt Policy: Speeches, Letters and State Papers* (New York: Current Literature Publications, 1908), vol. 2, p. 35.

30. *History of the Progressive Party, 1912–1916* (New York: New York University Press, 1958), p. 93.

31. Schlesinger and Israel, *American Presidential Elections*, vol. 3, p. 1,944.

32. *The Roosevelt Policy*, vol. 1, p. 79.

combinations which do good and those combinations which do evil."[33]

This moral evaluation of economic institutions symptomized the disintegration of nineteenth-century ideology. Corporations now had to show visibly that they were operating in the public interest. Public policy constituted both a threat and an opportunity for businessmen: they either had to demonstrate social responsibility or risk prosecution. Thus, federal antitrust policy directly influenced businessmen's ideology and practice and pointed to a new source of legitimacy. In emphasizing the importance of publicity in addressing the problem of the large corporation, Roosevelt had something in common with those he was to label the "muckrakers." The facts themselves were viewed as an agent of reform; they just needed exposure. As Roosevelt put it, "Daylight is a powerful discourager of evil."[34] The establishment of the Bureau of Corporations, with its investigatory and publicity powers, reflects this emphasis.

The goal of Roosevelt's antitrust policy was good trusts, not trust-busting. Historians, economists, and political scientists, noting the continuing process of consolidation during his administration, have pronounced Roosevelt's policy an inevitable failure. But this is to evaluate policy in terms of goals that were not those of the policy makers.[35] If we evaluate Roosevelt's policy by his own standards, our conclusions are much more favorable. Businessmen came to understand that Roosevelt was not opposed to all trusts. One of them conceded: "There is one great good that has come out of the Sherman Law and that is the agitation it has caused, the agitation on the question of what is moral or immoral in business."[36] In the first decade of the twentieth century, antitrust policy exposed the inadequacy of nineteenth-century business ideology and forced businessmen to reconsider their rules of conduct and their ways of conceptualizing social and economic institutions and relation-

33. Ibid., vol. 2, p. 463.
34. See *The Roosevelt Policy*, vol. 1, p. 38.
35. See Anderson, "The Logic of Public Problems," p. 30.
36. George W. Perkins, "The Sherman Law," Address before the Economic Club of Philadelphia, May 22, 1915.

ships. The Progressive notion of a good trust and management with good intentions was integrated into the new business ideology.

In 1911 both Standard Oil and the American Tobacco Company were found in violation of the Sherman Act by the Supreme Court. In the Standard Oil case, the intent behind consolidation became a significant factor in the Court's interpretation of antitrust law. Chief Justice Edward D. White concluded that the company intended "to drive others from the field and to exclude them from their right to trade."[37] In the American Tobacco case, the Court reviewed evidence showing that the company had bought other firms for the purpose of closing down their plants. The Court found the company in violation of the Sherman Act "not alone because of the dominion and control over the tobacco trade which actually exists, but because we think the conclusion of wrongful purpose and illegal combination is overwhelmingly established."[38] In the United States Steel Corporation case of 1920, the Court ruled consistently that market power, if not abused, did not in itself constitute a violation of antitrust law.

The election of Woodrow Wilson might have been expected to change the emphasis of antitrust proceedings. Wilson charged that his opponents in the election had been in league with business. "Mr. Roosevelt's conception of government is Mr. Taft's conception, that the Presidency of the United States is the presidency of a board of directors."[39] Wilson promised the country a "new freedom." He recognized that the old doctrine of individualistic competition predicated on small scale economic institutions was increasingly unrealistic. But his options in addressing the problem of the large corporation were restricted within the boundaries of contemporary political discourse. If the wholesale dissolution of corporations was ruled out, so, too, was the destruction of private corporate power through government ownership, for there lay Eugene Debs and the Socialists. The only remaining option was to take a reform of corporate practices as a policy goal, to be achieved by both exhortation

37. Standard Oil Company v. United States, 221 U.S. 76.
38. United States v. American Tobacco Company, 221 U.S. 182.
39. *The New Freedom* (New York: Doubleday, Page, 1913), p. 195.

and coercion. The aim was to encourage corporate officials to work actively in the public as well as the private interest—to make the "invisible hand" visible. It is not remarkable, therefore, that Wilson's view of the problem and his policy recommendations paralleled those of Roosevelt.

Wilson recognized that economic conditions had changed and that government had to be flexible in its response to these changes. "Our laws are still meant for business done by individuals; they have not been satisfactorily adjusted to business done by great combinations and we have got to adjust them," he wrote.[40] Like Roosevelt, Wilson emphasized that public authority was responsible for the existence of corporations, specifically rejecting the argument that the corporation constituted private property. "A modern joint stock corporation cannot in a proper sense be said to base its rights and powers upon the principles of private property. Its powers are wholly derived from legislation." The large corporation was "in a very proper sense everybody's business."[41] By eliminating the justifications provided by the private property argument and nineteenth-century ideology, public officials created further pressure for corporate officials to move toward social responsibility as a justification for corporate power.

For Wilson, consolidation was in keeping with the demands of economic efficiency and was therefore inevitable. However, some types of consolidation resulted from business "scheming" and were detrimental to the public interest. The distinction Wilson drew between "big business" and the "trusts" paralleled Roosevelt's distinction between "good" and "bad" trusts. "A trust is an arrangement to get rid of competition," he wrote, "and a big business is a business that has survived competition by conquering in the field of intelligence and economy."[42] To differentiate among large corporations on the basis of how they overcome competition appears somewhat contrived. Wilson suggested, in language reminiscent of social Darwinism, that surviving competition was an indication of

40. Ibid., p. 34.
41. Ibid., p. 132.
42. Ibid., p. 180.

proper economic conduct, but that the existence of a large corporation did not necessarily mean it had survived competition. Wilson was looking for a way to denounce the nastiness of, say, the
National Cash Register Company, which resorted to bribery and
sabotage to remove its competitors, without using Roosevelt's language of "good" and "bad" trusts. Like Roosevelt, Wilson saw publicity as a key policy tool, but in the 1912 campaign, Roosevelt
attempted to distinguish himself from Wilson and Taft by placing
a heavier emphasis on regulatory devices.

In 1913 the Pujo Committee published its investigation of the
corporate world. Under the chairmanship of Arsene Pujo, Democratic congressman from Louisiana, the House Committee on Banking and Currency revealed the extent of concentration in American
industry. J. P. Morgan, admitting to directorships in thirty-nine corporations, denied to the counsel for the committee that he wielded
power.

> Mr. Untermyer. That is your idea, is it? Your idea is that
> when a man has got a vast power, such as you have, you
> admit you have, do you not?
> Mr. Morgan. I do not know it, Sir.
> Mr. Untermyer. You admit you have, do you not?
> Mr. Morgan. I do not think I have.[43]

Louis D. Brandeis, litigious corporate critic and Progressive, commended the work of the committee. "The Pujo Committee has, in
the disclosure of the facts concerning financial concentration, made
a most important contribution toward attainment of the New Freedom." His approval derived from his own belief in the power of
publicity. "Sunlight is said to be the best of disinfectants; electric
light the most efficient policeman."[44]

In 1914 the Federal Trade Commission replaced the Bureau of
Corporations and the Clayton Act was passed. The commission was

43. U.S. Congress, House Committee on Banking and Currency, *Investigation
of Financial and Monetary Conditions in the United States under House Resolutions
Nos. 429 and 504* (Washington, D.C.: U.S. Government Printing Office, 1913),
p. 1,052.
44. *Other People's Money* (New York: Stokes, 1913), p. 92.

given the power to investigate corporations and request annual reports as well as other information. FTC investigations provided the basis for antitrust proceedings. The Clayton Act reinforced existing antitrust law with provisions against price discrimination, interlocking directorates, intercorporate stockholding, and other monopolistic practices.[45] In 1916 Wilson nominated Brandeis to the Supreme Court. One spokesman for business, Clarence W. Barron of the Boston News Bureau, wrote in an editorial entitled "An Unfit Appointment" that the "nomination of . . . Louis D. Brandeis to the United States Supreme Bench is an insult to New England and the business interests of the country."[46]

Businessmen may well have been insulted, particularly those who had been stung by Brandeis's activity against the big railroad companies, but they should not have been surprised by the nomination, which was consistent with the thrust of Wilson's antitrust policy. It was Brandeis, "the man whose opinions on economic questions [Wilson] respected above all others," who initially drew the president's attention to the political and economic problem that large corporations raised.[47] Brandeis himself, though he possessed, even cultivated, an image as the scourge of corporate institutions and their officials, belonged to the "corporation cure thyself" camp—though he was perhaps one of the more militant members. Brandeis, said Max Lerner, "has stood firmly for holding business enterprise rigorously to its social responsibilities."[48] Brandeis denied that there was a necessary conflict between capital and labor, believing that mutual interests tied them together. Aspects of Brandeis's thought, along with Wilson's and Roosevelt's, were incorporated into the new business ideology.

With Warren G. Harding's election in 1920, the emphasis on

45. See David D. Martin, *Mergers and the Clayton Act* (Berkeley: University of California Press, 1959), p. 3.

46. U.S. Congress, Senate, Subcommittee of the Committee on the Judiciary, *Hearings on the Nomination of Louis D. Brandeis*, 64th Cong., 1st sess. (Washington, D.C.: U.S. Government Printing Office, 1916), vol. 1, p. 123.

47. Arthur S. Link, *Woodrow Wilson and the Progressive Era* (New York: Harper and Bros., 1954), p. 48.

48. *Ideas as Weapons* (New York: Viking, 1939), p. 89.

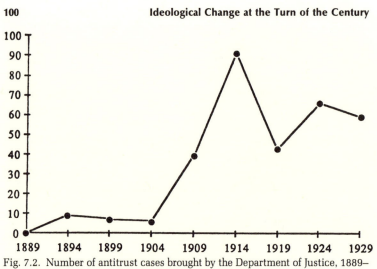

Fig. 7.2. Number of antitrust cases brought by the Department of Justice, 1889–1929

antitrust policy was reduced. Through various pieces of legislation, such as the Transportation Act of 1920 and the Capper-Volstead Act of 1922, consolidation became easier in some sectors of the economy, including the railroads and agricultural products. During the 1920s the salience of the corporation as a political issue diminished, although the Department of Justice continued to bring antitrust cases throughout the decade. Figure 7.2 indicates five-yearly totals of cases instituted by the department. This means of monitoring the development of the corporation as a political issue supports the analysis of party platforms. The take-off period occurred after the Northern Securities decision in 1904, and the peak of antitrust activity coincided with the high point of Progressivism in the 1910-14 period. Indeed, figures 7.1 and 7.2 chart the rise and fall of Progressivism as a social movement.

Antitrust policy gave a straightforward legal definition to the legitimacy of the large corporation. It indicates an autonomous role for the state; that is, state actions are not linked mechanistically to the demands of the business community, but are conditioned by the need to respond to popular demands. These popular demands act independently on the state to the extent that the business community is unsuccessful in framing them. Leading members of the business community in this era were quick to recognize the state's autonomy or "political adventurism." Robert Ozanne, in his history of International Harvester, remarks that a "trust lived always in the shadow of government sufferance. The Harvester corporation, after the initiation of the antitrust suit of 1911, was living by grace of the United States courts."[49] For the officials of large corporations, subject to governmental inquisitions, popular loathing, and possible dissolution, it was an uncomfortable and uncertain time. At the same time, as antitrust policy developed, it pointed to a source of new legitimacy for corporations. The paradox of threat and opportunity contained in antitrust policy in this period captures the essential ambivalence of Progressivism's relation to its bête noire, the large corporation.

It remains to be shown how the development of corporate legitimacy problems was connected to the content of ideological change in the business community. The link is the intellectual context within which these problems took shape. Legitimacy problems are more or less severe according to the number of social groups they affect: the more groups involved, the wider the range of demands being made on the affected institutions, and the greater the force behind these demands. As Walter Lippmann wrote:

> The trusts made enemies right and left: they squeezed the profits of the farmer, they made life difficult for the shopkeeper, they abolished jobbers and travelling salesmen, they closed down factories, they exercised an enormous control over credit through their size and through their eastern connections. Labor was no match for them, state legislatures were impotent before them. They came into the life of the simple American community as a tremendous revolutionary force, upsetting custom, changing men's status, demanding a readjustment for which people were unready.[50]

49. Ozanne, *McCormick and International Harvester,* p. 112.
50. *Drift and Mastery* (New York: Kennerly, 1914), p. 128.

From the Civil War to the second decade of the twentieth century, corporate legitimacy problems deepened. This process corresponded to the spread of discontent from the rural protests of the 1870s, directed primarily at the railroads, to the working class of the 1890s, to sections of the middle class in the 1900s. It accompanied industrialization. The willingness of these groups to challenge the power of corporations, and the timing of their protest, depended on a number of factors: the perceived directness of the threat to their socio-economic interests, the stage of group development and organization, the quality of leadership, and the availability of alternative ways of conceptualizing socio-economic relations. Unless alternatives are thought available, the outcome of such protest is typically resignation instead of rebellion.

The rejection of the old business ideology that began at the end of the nineteenth century and the development of Progressive thought at the beginning of the twentieth century provided the intellectual and conceptual context for the new business ideology. Ironically, the language of protest was adopted by those it was directed against.[51]

By 1900 there existed a comprehensive critique of traditional business ideology. This critique was the outcome of religious, literary, economic, and sociological attacks on classical economic theory, social Darwinism, and the economic institutions they justified. From these various perspectives, some common themes emerged: the benefits of cooperation rather than individualistic competition; social activism (defined in terms of both state and business action) rather than quietism; the socially dysfunctional consequences of great private wealth (the leisure class); and the theoretical and moral problems arising from an exclusive focus on self-interest.

Christian opposition to nineteenth-century business ideology coalesced in the Social Gospel movement. Selfishness, suffering, and conflict, necessary conditions for progress in this ideological scheme, appeared at odds with the Christian code. Social Gospelers looked to the private sector, not the state, for solutions. They "called

---

51. See Grant McConnell, *Private Power and American Democracy* (New York: Alfred A. Knopf, 1966), p. 32, and Weinstein, *The Corporate Ideal*, p. xiii.

for personal self-sacrifice, for a broader application of the principle of stewardship, for the voluntary adoption of such 'Christian' devices as profit sharing and cooperation."[52] Washington Gladden, a leader of the movement, raised the possibility of class harmony by arguing for solidarity between employers and employees. Businessmen themselves were, or at least had the opportunity of becoming, Gladden's agents of reform. "Such vast accumulations of power," he said, "cannot be left in the hands of soulless and conscienceless organizations. These corporations must find out whether they have souls or not. If they have souls and will demonstrate the fact by a conscientious administration of their trusts, there will be no disposition to interfere with them."[53]

The theme of cooperation was picked up by the economist Simon Patten, who argued that the American economy in this period was being transformed from a "pain economy" to a "pleasure economy." In the latter, "evolution was to be social rather than biological and cooperation rather than rivalry was to be the vehicle of evolutionary progress."[54] Laurence Gronlund, in his book *The Cooperative Commonwealth*, also advocated cooperation. Conceding that individualism had "done civilization excellent service," he argued that its day was over and the era of social cooperation would follow. "The social organism, like a harmoniously developed individual, has three stages of growth; implicit obedience, restless self-assertion, and, finally, intelligent cooperation."[55] The state, in Gronlund's view, would foster cooperation through its control over the economy.

Edward Bellamy, in his utopian novel *Looking Backward*, contrasted the social solidarity and cooperation of the future with the conflict and strife of 1880s America through the eyes of Julian West, who awakes from a 113-year hypnotic trance in the year 2000. The book argued that consolidation was economically justified and described a future in which the state managed industry in the public

52. Fine, *Laissez Faire*, p. 179.

53. *Social Facts and Forces* (1897; reprint, Port Washington, N.Y.: Kennikat, 1971), p. 113.

54. See E. K. Hunt, "Simon N. Patten's Contributions to Economics," *Journal of Economic Issues* 4 (December 1970), p. 38.

55. *The Cooperative Commonwealth* (London: William Reeves, 1884), p. 57.

interest. Production on a huge scale was very efficient and also easy for state officials to administer. "The machine which they direct is indeed a vast one, but so logical in its principles and direct and simple in its workings, that it all but runs itself."[56] Bellamy's book was very popular, but neither its sentiments nor the various calls for cooperation carried much weight with businessmen at the time. In 1894 thirteen "armies of unemployed," with Bellamy's support, marched on Washington. Concerned that one of the company's trains might be commandeered by the unemployed, an official of the Northwestern Railroad in Iowa said that if this happened "he would send a wild engine with the throttle open to meet it." He conjectured that "the wreck will solve the problem as to whether we are obliged to carry these men without remuneration."[57] A few years later Jack London was to paint a bleak picture of the immediate future in The Iron Heel, in which private corporate wealth became the basis for totalitarian dictatorship.

While Bellamy, Gronlund, and the Socialists argued for comprehensive state control of industry, others made sectoral distinctions in deciding where private ownership should be replaced by public ownership. Richard T. Ely argued that corporations in industries that constituted "natural monopolies," such as the railways and the utilities, were most likely to abuse their power. Public ownership was appropriate in such cases; to attempt to enforce competition would be economically inefficient. In arguing the case for public ownership, he pointed to the results of private ownership. "Instances are numerous where railways have so regulated rates as to kill one town and build up another as they saw fit."[58] Ely argued that private property should be viewed as a social institution, not an absolute right, and that its possession should depend on "the welfare of society." The doctrine of eminent domain had been used, but to the benefit of the railways themselves in securing passage for the tracks where private properties had presented an obstacle.

56. Looking Backward (1888; reprint, Cambridge, Mass.: Harvard University Press, 1967), p. 212.

57. Dorfman, Thorstein Veblen, p. 105.

58. Outlines of Economics (New York: Chautauqua Century Press, 1893), p. 60.

Economies-of-scale arguments for corporate size and power were also inadequate. Critics like Ely conceded that large institutions were justified economically, while at the same time arguing that they did not need to be left in private hands. The ideological problem for officials of these corporations was to show why private control was preferable.

Ely's work represents a systematic and interesting critique of classical political economy and its economic and political consequences. He identified himself with the German "Historical School" of political economy; not Marx, but Bruno Hildebrand, Carl Knies, and Wilhelm Roscher were its key figures. In opposing the English or classical political economy, they asserted the temporal and spatial boundedness of economic theory. They rejected grand generalizations. Ely wrote that the classical economists, because they lacked such an historical approach, "discerned, often with great clearness, some of the forces then at work in economic life . . . But while some of these were fundamental and permanent others were scarcely more than the accidents of their day."[59] Because it recognized that it was inappropriate to apply classical political economy to contemporary economic and social conditions, "this younger political economy no longer permits the science to be used as a tool in the hands of the greedy and avaricious for keeping down and oppressing the laboring classes."[60]

Others noted the ideological (legitimizing) function of classical economic theory—what Joan Robinson has called "the ideology to end ideology"—and its quietistic implications.[61] A version of Malthus's doctrine, Gronlund wrote, was "hatched in the salons of the wealthy and tenderly nursed there because it relieves the conscience of the ruling classes from all responsibility for the misery which surrounds them."[62] Henry Demarest Lloyd claimed that the "doctrines of the desire of wealth, of exclusive regulation by competition, and of the irresistible laws of trade have been a royal road

59. Ibid., p. 75.

60. Ely, *The Past and Present of Political Economy* (Baltimore: Johns Hopkins University Press, 1884), p. 64.

61. Joan Robinson, *Economic Philosophy* (Chicago: Aldine, 1962), p. 53.

62. Gronlund, *The Cooperative Commonwealth*, p. 98.

for shifting responsibility for injustice and legal selfishness from human shoulders upon the back of Nature."[63] And Henry George, proclaiming that "the association of poverty with progress is the great enigma of our time," said that "the Malthusian doctrine parries the demand for reform, and shelters selfishness from question and from conscience by the interposition of inevitable necessity."[64]

Ely carried his criticism of classical economic theory to its basic psychological assumption. He denied the supremacy of self-interest in social and economic activity, as well as its theoretical and moral value; such motives as national honor, devotion to principles, and altruism were also significant. He further argued that the "ideal of economic life is then the union of self-interest and altruism in a broad humanitarian spirit."[65] Lloyd, too, questioned the emphasis on self-interest. He said that Adam Smith himself, while espousing the virtues of self-interest, jeopardized his fortune with his kindness.[66] The critical device of contrasting the theoretician's actions with his propositions was also used against Malthus, who was charged incorrectly with having personally compounded the population problem by fathering eleven children.[67]

The corruption of government by private corporations was Lloyd's theme. He described, for example, the "orgy of the sugar trust and Congress, out of which the tariff bill of 1894 was born."[68] Such scandals served to raise questions about the social Darwinist assumption of the social utility of great private wealth. Lester Ward, a great optimist about the potential of social science research in the struggle for social reform, described the very wealthy as "the parasitic classes of human society."[69] This was the era of the robber

63. "The Political Economy of Seventy-three Million Dollars," *The Atlantic Monthly,* July, 1882, p. 74.

64. *Progress and Poverty* (New York: Robert Schalkenbach Foundation, 1942), p. 99.

65. *Political Economy,* p. 35.

66. "The Political Economy of Seventy-three Million Dollars," p. 71.

67. Gronlund, *The Cooperative Commonwealth,* p. 98.

68. *Wealth Against Commonwealth* (New York: Harper and Bros., 1894), p. 449.

69. *Dynamic Sociology* (1883; reprint, New York: Greenwood, 1968), vol. I, p. 595.

barons, in which dinner guests were served oysters complete with the pearl and after dinner smoked cigarettes wrapped in hundred-dollar bills.[70] Thorstein Veblen railed against these representatives of the "leisure class," whose function "in social evolution is to retard the movement and to conserve what is obsolescent."[71] But their attitude toward wealth was one of conspicuous destruction as much as conspicuous consumption. About the same time that Veblen was reporting the habits of the industrial rich, Franz Boas, on the same continent, was observing the Kwakiutl Indians and their penchant for publicly destroying wealth in the "potlatch." Indeed, Veblen could be regarded as an anthropologist as easily as an economist.

The old business ideology was based on an economic theory that was too abstract and whose policy consequences were too brutal to engender continued acceptance. The rejection of the ideology as a justification for corporations, however, did not amount to a rejection of these institutions as such. There was general agreement among critics that large business operations and consolidation were economic necessities. Aside from the Socialists, critics directed their attacks at contemporary corporate leaders. In detailing the abuse of corporate power, they implied that there could be a proper use for it. Ely's call for a humanitarian spirit in business anticipated the Progressive distinction between "good" and "bad" trusts.

The significance of the Progressive era, beginning around 1900, is not that it represented a new order of criticism, but rather that the existing criticisms were transformed into popular beliefs. The muckrakers held up an unfavorable picture of the corporations for all to see. Ida Tarbell exposed the methods Standard Oil had employed to achieve its great size, while Lincoln Steffens diagnosed the poisonous effect of business on the body politic.

The typical business man is a bad citizen; he is busy. If he is a "big business man" and very busy, he does not ne-

70. Matthew Josephson, *The Robber Barons* (New York: Harcourt Brace, 1934), p. 338.

71. *The Theory of the Leisure Class* (1899; reprint, Boston: Houghton Mifflin, 1973), p. 137.

glect, but he is busy with politics . . . I found him buying boodlers in St. Louis, defending grafters in Minneapolis, originating corruption in Pittsburgh, sharing with bosses in Philadelphia, deploring reform in Chicago, and beating good government with corruption funds in New York. He is a self-righteous fraud, this big business man."[72]

These accounts of business practices reached, for the period, huge audiences. The magazines that published them had a total circulation of more than three million.[73] Upton Sinclair's vivid description of the disgusting working conditions and standards in the Chicago meat industry produced a public outcry and federal food statutes, and was translated into seventeen languages. According to Hans Thorelli, the muckrakers "contributed heavily to the fact that the problems of big business and industrial combination and competition retained a place at or near the top of the nation's agenda from Roosevelt's first administration to the outbreak of World War I."[74]

Questioning the legitimacy of private corporations was the central theme of Progressivism. United in their opposition to corporate power, Progressives split over their proposals for reform. Those who took nineteenth-century business ideology seriously argued for a reassertion of individualistic competition and the break up of large concentrations of capital. Others, whose views predominated in the development of public policy, argued that corporations should be converted rather than destroyed. Intellectuals associated with this wing of Progressivism include Herbert Croly and Stephen Duncan-Clark. Large private corporations and their officials, according to Croly, had "become too wealthy and powerful for their official standing in American life;" they had "not obeyed the laws."[75]

72. The Shame of the Cities (1904; reprint, New York: Peter Smith, 1948), p. 5.

73. C. C. Regier, The Era of the Muckrakers (Gloucester, Mass.: Peter Smith, 1957), p. 196.

74. The Federal Antitrust Policy (Baltimore: Johns Hopkins University Press, 1953), p. 334.

75. The Promise of American Life (1909; reprint, Cambridge, Mass.: Harvard University Press, 1965), p. 116.

Among other things, Croly suggested that one way to address the problem of corporate power was "industrial self-governing democracy." He maintained that the worker's claim to have a say in the conditions of his employment paralleled the citizen's claims to have a say (by voting) in government policy. Although union strength increased during this period, peaking in 1920 with approximately five million union members in the American work force, the union movement was not to be the vehicle for Croly's industrial democracy. His view of how reform should be accomplished can be regarded as a kind of industrial Fabianism. He looked to a few dedicated employers to initiate reform. The "enlightened and wilful employers," whom he expected to overcome the conflictual nature of industrial relations, must voluntarily restrain their pursuit of profit, at least in the short term, in order to establish a democratic reconstruction of their institutions.[76] Croly expected their sacrifice to have longer-term rewards with respect to employee productivity and efficiency. He thought that industrial democracy might make workers more amenable to the discipline of scientific management. Walter Lippmann, a member of Croly's editorial staff on the New Republic, detected at this time the emergence of a group of disinterested employers. Businessmen, he said, were "talking more and more about their 'responsibilities,' and their 'stewardship.' It is the swan-song of the old commercial profiteering and a dim recognition that the motives in business are undergoing a revolution."[77]

Not surprisingly, the contemporary politician whom Croly most admired was Theodore Roosevelt. In his introduction to Stephen Duncan-Clark's book The Progressive Movement, published in 1913, Roosevelt highly recommended it as a statement of the principles of Progressivism. Duncan-Clark called on employers to recognize their social responsibilities. Consolidation of capital was a product of industrial evolution and necessary to economic development. "To the Progressive the trust is not an evil to be eradicated but a potential good to be developed."[78] The large corporation, for this wing

76. Croly, Progressive Democracy (New York: Macmillan, 1914), pp. 393–94.
77. Lippmann, Drift and Mastery, p. 23.
78. The Progressive Movement (Boston: Small, Maynard, 1913), p. 29.

of the Progressive movement, was the institutional form of the moment; all that it needed was proper direction. Duncan-Clark emphasized the serious legitimacy problems facing businessmen. "The alert and intelligent member of the capitalist group is aware of the fact that he and his class are under surveillance today; that they are distrusted by many of the people, and that the situation demands, not an arrogant defiance of this irrational attitude, but an earnest effort to justify their place in the social organism."[79] Like Croly, Duncan-Clark saw employers themselves as agents for reform. He predicted the triumph of "cooperation" in industrial life.

Reformist criticism of the corporation by the Progressives and their forerunners presented both threats and opportunities to corporate officials. While exposing abuses of power, critics allowed businessmen themselves a major role in the process of reform. Thus, employers had a chance to adjust their activities before their power was circumscribed by external constraints. By contrast, the Fabians and other European reformers relied much more heavily on state action. The emergence of a disinterested capitalist (instead of administrative) class, or at least one that could combine the pursuit of self-interest with altruistic motives, became a key tenet of the new business ideology and inspired the self-conscious development of business as a "profession."

Although this chapter has concentrated on the external pressures that contributed to corporate legitimacy problems and the transformation of business ideology, this is not to deny that there were also internal factors related to the transformation of business ideology. It should not be surprising that businessmen themselves had difficulties in adjusting to the rise of the corporation. The new facts of business life did not fit easily into the old way of seeing the economic world. The nineteenth-century business ideology was adrift from reality. Businessmen faced, in a sense, a personal crisis of legitimacy. Charles Schwab of Bethlehem Steel provides a disarming description of such a crisis: "When the investigations of capital and the organization of great companies were taking place, I commenced to feel a good deal disturbed, and with all the agitation in

79. Ibid., p. 216.

the press commenced to feel that perhaps I had participated in something that was sinful and dishonest, and all sorts of things. I am a good Catholic."[80]

Businessmen needed to make sense of their environment and to provide new answers for their critics. They also needed to know that their work was of social value. Greed alone had never been enough. Max Weber has shown how their forebears relied on the inspiration that they were doing God's work in their struggle with the aristocracy. The robber barons at least could claim to have begun with nothing and individually struggled to the top. Of Jay Gould, Jim Fisk, J. P. Morgan, Philip Armour, Andrew Carnegie, James Hill, John Rockefeller, Collis Huntington, Leland Stanford, and Jay Cooke, only Morgan, the son of a banker, did not have a childhood "darkened by poverty," according to Matthew Josephson. All of these men, Josephson wrote, "showed promising signs of shiftiness and self-reliance in boyhood."[81] In contrast, a systematic survey of leading big businessmen and their social origins in the 1920s found that most were the sons of businessmen.[82] The robber barons, representing a final fling for the private selfishness–public good formula, provided dubious authority for the corporate officials who replaced them. It was no longer even primarily their own property that they were "risking" in situations of oligopoly or monopoly. They not only needed to prove the legitimacy of their power to others, they also needed to prove it to themselves. Thus, psychological factors were incorporated into the process of ideological change. The confluence of external and internal pressures marked the transition from selfishness to social responsibility. Of course, this ideological change was not total; the old ideas based on classical economic theory were not extinguished. They retained their grip on the minds of small businessmen in the 1920s, and have periodically resurged since then.

---

80. "Capital and Labor," *Annals of the American Academy* 81 (January 1919), p. 157.

81. *The Robber Barons*, p. 33.

82. F. W. Taussig and C. S. Joslyn, *American Business Leaders* (New York: Macmillan, 1932), p. 234.

eight

Remaking the American Capitalist Class III: The New Business Ideology

The main components of the new business ideology—which we may call "progressive" to acknowledge its link to Progressive thought—were cooperation, service, social responsibility, trusteeship, efficiency, and power. Although these concepts are functionally interdependent, they represent distinguishable components for the purpose of analysis.[1] This chapter will describe how the aims and rules of business conduct changed as businessmen attempted to show that their private direction of powerful industrial institutions contributed to the public interest. The analysis is based on businessmen's writings and the observations of business journalists and academics during the 1920s. The question of how unemployment, poverty, and financial provision for old age were transformed into problems to be dealt with by corporations will be addressed, and an effort will be made to evaluate the effectiveness of Progressive ideology in providing corporations with legitimacy.

Reinhard Bendix connects the change in business ideology to the process of bureaucratization that corporations were undergoing at this time. He contrasts the pre–World War I era, when social Darwinist imagery of combat and struggle dominated business thought, with the postwar emphasis on cooperation and peaceful

---

1. See Philip Converse, "The Nature of Belief Systems in Mass Publics," in David Apter, ed., *Ideology and Discontent* (New York: Free Press, 1964), p. 207.

industrial relations. Herman Krooss, surveying the views of a selection of big businessmen in the 1920s, notes a rhetorical shift
away from profit: "Any mention of profits was regarded as vulgar,
and any admission of a desire for profits was regarded as anti-
social." On the other hand, James Prothro—relying on organizations
like the National Association of Manufacturers and the U.S. Cham-
ber of Commerce as sources for business thought—finds a renewed
emphasis on values associated with the nineteenth-century ideology.[2] However, many commentators in the 1920s pointed to the radical change that had taken place in the preceding twenty years or
so. The notion that business had fundamentally changed was itself
part of the Progressive ideology, as a brief sampling of writings of
the period demonstrates:

> Mankind's conception of industry has, in very recent
> years, undergone a revolution. It has not yet penetrated to
> all corners of the structure . . . There are still men near
> the top, who shortsightedly conceive of industry as a
> mere means to personal power and cash profits . . . But
> there is a far larger proportion of men who think sanely.[3]

> The narrowly individualistic attitude toward business and
> social problems that formerly prevailed is being outgrown.
> Businessmen generally are adopting a broader approach to
> such questions and are recognizing their responsibilities
> to other groups in society as well as to their own
> employees.[4]

> Signs are not wanting that a new spirit has come into
> business. The many gifts left to education and philan-
> thropy, the various successful plans in profit-sharing and

2. Bendix, *Work and Authority*, p. 285; Krooss, *Executive Opinion: What
Business Leaders Said and Thought on Economic Issues, 1920–1960* (New York:
Doubleday, 1970), p. 41; Prothro, *The Dollar Decade: Business Ideas in the 1920s*
(Baton Rouge: Louisiana State University Press, 1954), pp. 212–19.

3. "Manpower, Horsepower, and the New Industrial Leadership," *Industrial
Management* (December 1926), p. 333.

4. National Industrial Conference Board, *Industrial Relations: Policies and
Programs* (New York, 1931), p. 6.

cooperation, the very considerable raise in wages and the granting of bonuses—each is an indication of an increasing social responsibility.[5]

Advocacy of a regime of low wages as a national economic philosophy has passed out with horse cars, hoop skirts and the league opposed to woman suffrage.[6]

Prior to the war, industry was considered as being primarily conducted for profit, the theory being that by competition, and by the free play of selfish, economic forces the greatest advantages to the greatest number—labor, capital, and the public—would be accomplished. After the war, the idea gained ground and grew in force and acceptance, that in reality industry was a social institution.[7]

This new business man is essentially a statesman. This new business man looks up on his private business as his best instrument of public service. He believes that he can render a greater public service by being statesmanlike during office hours than by being philanthropic after office hours.[8]

Carnegie's assertion that public service concerns arose after one had acquired wealth was transcended in the Progressive business ideology by the idea that such concerns arose in the process of acquiring wealth.

At the conceptual core of the Progressive business ideology was cooperation. Businessmen rejected the social Darwinist and classical economic language of competition in favor of its opposite. Samuel Untermyer, the perspicacious counsel for the Pujo commit-

5. Rudolph M. Binder, *Major Social Problems* (New York: Prentice-Hall, 1921), p. 190.

6. Merryle S. Rukeyser, "Real Wages at High Peak: Will They Last?" *Forbes*, February 15, 1927, p. 13.

7. W. Jett Lauck, *Political and Industrial Democracy, 1776–1926* (New York: Funk and Wagnalls, 1926), p. 42.

8. Glenn Frank, "Needed: A New Man of Business," *The Magazine of Business*, November 1927, p. 567.

tee, uncovered this change in his interrogation of an evasive J. P. Morgan.

> Mr. Untermyer. You are opposed to competition, are you not?
> Mr. Morgan. No; I do not mind competition.
> Mr. Untermyer. You would rather have combination, would you not?
> Mr. Morgan. Yes.
> Mr. Untermyer. You are an advocate of combination and cooperation, as against competition, are you not?
> Mr. Morgan. Yes; cooperation I should favor.[9]

Cooperation meant, at one level, cooperation between formerly competing units. "Competition is warfare and tends to excesses . . . The cure for the evils of excessive competition is cooperation."[10] The corporation represented the institutional embodiment of cooperation. While advocating cooperation, businessmen denounced ruthless competitive methods as leading to immoral business practices in the selfish pursuit of private gain, not the public interest.[11]

At another level, cooperation embraced capital, labor, and the community. The Social Gospelers had received an audience in the business community. The basis of this cooperation was an assumed mutuality of interests. The various parties to industrial production would achieve higher efficiency, from which all would benefit, by avoiding conflict. Charles M. Schwab, chairman of Bethlehem Steel, argued before the American Society of Mechanical Engineers that managers and labor should recognize that "conflict between capital and labor is destructive of the interests of each; that it is unnec-

9. U.S. Congress, House Committee on Banking and Currency, *Investigation of Financial and Monetary Conditions in the United States under House Resolutions Nos. 429 and 504* (Washington, D.C.: U.S. Government Printing Office, 1913), p. 1,050.

10. Walter S. Gifford, "Can Prosperity be Managed?" *Saturday Evening Post,* November 8, 1930, p. 13.

11. George W. Perkins, "Business and Government," *The Saturday Evening Post,* March 16, 1912, p. 22.

essary and mutually expensive."[12] J. Ward Moorehouse, the public relations man in John Dos Passos's *U.S.A.*, has a similar vision of

> American industry like a steamengine, like a high-power
> locomotive on a great express train charging through the
> night of old individualistic methods . . . What does a steam-
> engine require? Cooperation, coordination of the inven-
> tor's brain, the promotor's brain that made the
> development of these high-power products possible . . .
> Coordination of capital, the storedup energy of the race
> . . . labor, the prosperous contented American working
> man to whom the unprecedented possibilities of capital
> collected in great corporations had given the full dinner
> pail, cheap motor transport, insurance, short working
> hours . . . a measure of comfort and prosperity unequaled
> before or since in the tragic procession of recorded his-
> tory.[13]

While cooperation promised greater economic efficiency, it also was a recognition that others besides the representatives of capital had an interest in the corporate decision making process, even that they had "political" rights.

Mackenzie King, personal advisor to John D. Rockefeller, Jr., viewed the corporation as an association of capital, labor, and the community. He claimed that there was "no defence possible on grounds of democratic theory or fundamental justice" for the inordinate weight given capital in the decision making process.[14] Rockefeller himself said that "representation is a principle which is fundamentally just and vital to the successful conduct of industry. It means, broadly speaking, democracy through cooperation, as contrasted with autocracy."[15] Cooperation constituted a response to Progressive criticism of the antidemocratic nature of corporations, as well as reflecting disenchantment with "ruthless competition."

12. "Human Engineering," *Law and Labor* 10 (January 1928), p. 14.

13. *U.S.A.* (New York: Modern Library, 1930), p. 267.

14. *Industry and Humanity* (New York: Houghton Mifflin, 1918), p. 370.

15. *The Personal Relation in Industry* (New York: Boni and Liveright, 1923), p. 20.

This new vocabulary enjoined businessmen to certain policies. Co-operation implied worker participation in decision making. Robert S. Brookings advocated employee representation schemes as "another way in which corporation managements can do something to encourage and justify a cooperative attitude on the part of labor."[16]

This new conception of industrial relationships was further reflected in efforts to enable employees to become stockholders. In so doing, it was claimed, workers were given access to the traditional locus of corporate power. Thomas N. Carver wrote that "the joint stock corporation always was, in theory, a democratic institution. For several reasons it failed, in the past, to be democratic in practice. It is now actually becoming, in practice as well as in theory, a democratic institution."[17] Herbert Hoover was "convinced that one of the continuous and underlying problems of sustained democracy [was] the constant and wider diffusion of property ownership"[18] George M. Verity elaborated on this theme in an article entitled "The Unseen Business Revolution."

> To my mind it is morally certain that, unless there had been a radical change in the ethical standards and mutual interest policies of commerce and industry over and above what they were twenty-five years ago, there never could or would have been such a marvellous development of the stockholding partnership relation that now exists in the large business structures of the country, which represent such a gigantic scheme of cooperation between our people and the organized business of the nation.[19]

Cooperation conferred democratic rights in certain areas of decision making upon parties other than management, thus blurring the distinction between capitalists and workers. It also conveyed the idea that managers should occupy a more general "trustee" position, with "social responsibilities" to various constituencies.

16. *Industrial Ownership* (New York: Macmillan, 1925), p. 65.
17. "The Diffusion of Ownership," Academy of Political Science, *Proceedings* 11, no. 3 (1925), p. 40.
18. "The Diffusion of Property Ownership," ibid., p. 137.
19. *The Iron Age* (February 25, 1926), p. 543.

Charles Schwab argued that "cooperation requires leadership in industry that regards itself not as a partisan but as a trustee, striving to guide the efforts of both capital and labor into profitable channels."[20] Axtell Byles, president of the Tide Water Association Oil Company, described oil executives as "professional business managers" who were "running a large part of the business of America as trustees for its people."[21] Sam A. Lewisohn, vice president of Miami Copper Company and chairman of the American Management Association, said: "The principal factor in industrial harmony is the leadership of the employer . . . The problem is largely that of securing a new emotional orientation toward the subject on the part of our employers and our executives."[22] Wallace B. Donham, dean of the Harvard Business School, claimed that the "big corporation in its natural development inevitably tends to higher ethical standards, to more of a feeling of trusteeship for the community and for the employee as well as for security holders."[23] Charles Steinmetz of General Electric linked corporate social responsibility to the growth of business that the corporation represented. Noting "the joint productive activity of many thousands of employees," he argued that "a social responsibility, and with it a social duty, arises in the corporation, and the corporation can no more be entirely private property." According to Steinmetz, this fact was "fully recognized by all the more progressive and thus more successful corporations" and was the basis of "the rapidly increasing activities of the corporation in social relations with their employees, [and] with the public at large."[24]

Cooperation, democratic rights, trusteeship, and social responsibility entailed a reconceptualization of the status of wage labor. It was no longer treated as a commodity, but as a human activity.

20. "Human Engineering," p. 14.

21. "Conditions in the Oil Industry," *Review of Reviews* 7 (March 1929), p. 69.

22. "Management: A Behavior Problem," *The Survey* 56 (September 1, 1926), p. 565.

23. "The Professional Side of Training," in Henry Metcalf, ed., *Business Management as a Profession* (Chicago: Shaw, 1927), p. 225.

24. *America and the New Epoch* (New York: Harper and Bros., 1916), p. 200.

Businessmen and commentators self-consciously talked of the "human factor in industry." For Oscar Newfang, the way to harmony between labor and capital was to realize "that labor is not a commodity" and "that capital is a commodity."[25] The new industrial era, another writer said, was "characterized by efforts to eliminate strife between capital and labor, to make the workers' lot easier, and to establish true and fair relationships between employer and employee—in short to make industry more human."[26] Owen D. Young, chairman of General Electric, in discussing employee stock ownership, looked forward "to the day when human beings who gave their lives to the job—if you want to call that labor—will be the employer and capital will be the commodity which they buy for their own account."[27] Even the Democratic party platforms of 1920, 1924, and 1928 specifically declared: "Labor is not a commodity; it is human."

Businessmen signified their recognition of the human factor and the cooperative nature of business by providing workers with life insurance, medical facilities, leisure and recreational activities, pensions, and unemployment benefits. According to George Perkins, "If profit sharing, pensions, insurance, and the like mean anything, they must mean cooperation between capital and labor—cooperation in the broadest, most helpful and enduring form."[28] The Progressive business ideology provided new standards for businessmen to evaluate the nature of the corporation and its relationship to society. By crediting management with the discretion and the power to address social issues, the new business ideology made business's relationship with society more problematical, in the literal sense of increasing the number of social problems facing business. Instead of accepting the labor contract and its social consequences as externally determined by market forces, businessmen like Schwab now asked:

25. *Harmony between Labor and Capital* (New York: Putnam's, 1927), p. 92.
26. W. R. Winans, "What Employee Publications Are Doing to Improve Industrial Relations," *Industrial Management* (April 1925), p. 212.
27. Quoted in B. C. Forbes, "Labour to Become Capital! Owen D. Young's Vision," *Forbes*, December 1, 1927, p. 9.
28. Quoted in Ozanne, *McCormick and International Harvester*, p. 73.

What are these reasonable wants of employees, which
they have a right to see satisfied as far as conditions of
industry permit? I believe they include the payment of
fair wages for efficient services; steady, uninterrupted employment; safeguarding of their lives and health; good
physical working conditions; a voice in the regulation of
conditions under which they work; provision for them to
lay up savings and to become partners in the business
through stock ownership; and finally, some guarantee of
financial independence in old age.[29]

Unemployment in the old business ideology was certainly not a
responsibility of businessmen, or even something they could do
much about. It was a recurring condition of the labor market caused
by a disequilibrium between supply and demand, which the consequence of a fall in the price for labor would correct. Inasmuch as
unemployment was designated as a problem at all in the old business ideology, it was attributed to the personal, often moral, characteristics of the unemployed. In the new ideology, as Elbert H. Gary
wrote, the problem of unemployment was "essentially one of business and of business management, and must be met by business
statesmanship through the normal channels of business and economic organization."[30] Sam Lewisohn declared, "As the direction
of the affairs of the business world lies mainly in the hands of
employing management and of financiers, it is obvious that the responsibility of taking the initiative in adopting measures to mini-
mize unemployment is primarily theirs."[31] Henry S. Dennison
disputed the inevitability of unemployment caused by business
depression. "Not only have practical ways been found to prevent
seasonal unemployment, but measures have also been taken to min-
imize cyclical unemployment and to relieve the worker from its
disastrous effects."[32] Herman Feldman concluded that "if one looks

29. Schwab, "Human Engineering," p. 14.
30. "Unemployment and Business," *Harper's Magazine*, June 1915, p. 71.
31. Quoted in Herman Feldman, *The Regularization of Employment* (New
York: Harper and Bros., 1925), p. 68.
32. "To Cut the Waste of Unemployment," *The Nation's Business* 12 (October
1924), p. 32.

behind the numerous conditions that result in irregular employment ... the outstanding circumstance is the spirit of management."[33]

James W. Hook argued not only that businessmen had an obligation to prevent unemployment, but also that they might prevent
the state from becoming involved in this policy area. "American
industry can and must solve the national unemployment problem
if compulsory public unemployment insurance is to be avoided ...
[Income maintenance for workers in depressions] is the direct and
pressing obligation of industry ... The cry of rugged individualism
would be a compelling one if all our citizens are endowed with
equal opportunities and equal abilities. But we are not so endowed."[34] Other commentators noted a change in attitude toward
unemployment. "American thinking had grasped the fact by 1911
that only a small proportion of unemployment was due to the personal deficiencies of the unemployed." By 1921, when President
Harding called the first federal Conference on Unemployment, the
problem was viewed as "partly due to defects in business management and partly to deep underlying forces in the business world."[35]

Consistent with the new ideology, businessmen endorsed the
Progressive demand that corporate activities be publicized. "Social
responsibility" implies that those to whom one is responsible know
how that responsibility is being exercised; business "must be done
in glass pockets." This endorsement shows the extent to which the
concept of the corporation as private property had broken down in
businessmen's own minds, and how the "old days of secretiveness
and the public-be-damned spirit in corporate management had gone
by, never to return."[36]

33. Feldman, *The Regularization of Employment* (New York: Harper and Bros.,
1925), p. 63.
34. "Industry's Obligations to the Unemployed," *The Iron Age* (August 20,
1931), p. 511.
35. Commons, *History of Labor*, vol. 3, p. 152.
36. Thomas W. Lamont, "Publicity for Industrial Corporations," *Industrial
Management* (July 1927). See also George Perkins's testimony before the House
Committee on Banking and Currency (1913) and Elbert H. Gary, "The Public
be Informed," *The World's Work* 53 (December 1926).

In the progressive ideology, profit was de-emphasized as a goal for businessmen. "We have had among us those who have worked for money alone," said Charles Schwab, "but they have been merely beach combers who, when wreckage was scarce, connived at or brought about wrecks. They have never headed large constructive corporations."[37] Some of the Progressive business ideologues counterposed "service" to profit. "The man who imagines that the be-all and the end-all of business is to enrich himself is on the wrong track," declared an editorial in *Forbes* magazine. "First seek to serve, and rewards will follow."[38] John D. Rockefeller, Jr., wrote: "The soundest industrial policy is that which has constantly in mind the welfare of the employees as well as the making of profits, and which, when human considerations demand it, subordinates profit to welfare."[39]

The most fervent ideologues depicted the changes in business thought and practice in terms of a religious conversion. *Harper's Magazine* in 1925 seriously asked whether there was "more of the spirit of Christianity in the Catholic Church, the Methodist Church, Harvard College, the Standard Oil Company, or the Steel Trust?"[40] Clarence Birdseye said that corporate pension or health schemes were "a manifestation of the corporate soul."[41] Burton Konkle claimed that the corporation had "begun to give evidence of spiritual qualities."[42] And Arthur Nash, a Cincinnati businessman who gave $600,000 of stock in his company to his employees in order to avoid becoming a millionaire and who thought of Jesus as a "carpenter-contractor," argued that Christianity meant a socially responsible attitude to employees. "We cannot conceive of Him asking one of His employees to do a job which would involve his

37. "What Does Business Want from the Government?" *Colliers*, December 11, 1920, p. 7.

38. *Forbes*, October 15, 1924, p. 70.

39. *The Personal Relation in Industry*, p. 11.

40. Edward S. Martin, "Shall Business Run the World?" *Harper's Magazine*, February 1925, p. 378.

41. "Have Corporations Moral Natures?" *Outlook* 109 (March 31, 1915), p. 786.

42. "Can Organizations Have Souls?" *Forum* 79 (May 1928), p. 705.

being destroyed in the doing of it ... And the time has come, as
the mind of the Man of Galilee is being revealed afresh to the world,
that industry must stop using men and women to make money and
go to using money to make men and women."[43]
A theme of Progressive business ideology was that service would
be rewarded by profit. The obligations of social responsibility were
made easier to assume with an economic incentive; payoffs would
come from a more peaceful and contented work force. Henry Ford
wrote: "Well-conducted business enterprise cannot fail to return a
profit, but profit must and inevitably will come as reward for good
service. It cannot be the basis—it must be the result of service."[44]
A businessman who made the argument most vigorously was Edward A. Filene.

> The new principles are gaining headway because they are
> demonstrably more practical and more profitable than the
> assumptions about which the old capitalism was organ-
> ized ... This new capitalism is looking for profits as ea-
> gerly as the old capitalism ever did, but it is seeking these
> profits by diametrically opposite means. Instead of mak-
> ing wages as low and prices as high as possible, it is mak-
> ing prices as low and wages as high as possible. The new
> capitalism makes its profits by shortening the work-day of
> the workers ... The new capitalism is making profits
> through cultivating and extending the principles of coop-
> eration.[45]

That many corporate social policies were cut back in the 1921
depression indicated that many businessmen did not consider the
economic benefits of social policies sufficiently tangible to continue
them during hard times.

Proponents of the new ideology argued that it was in a businessman's self-interest to pay high wages in order to increase demand. "A cut in real wages would eliminate part of the effective

43. *The Golden Rule in Business* (New York: Revell, 1923), p. 125.
44. *My Life and Work* (New York: Doubleday, Page, 1922), p. 20.
45. "New Capitalism," *The Annals of the American Academy of Political and
Social Science* (May 1930), pp. 4–5.

demand . . . and would cause a serious crisis in American business
. . . There is no longer an important capitalistic group waiting for
a propitious moment to deflate labor," wrote Merryle Ruckeyser.[46]
However, this line of reasoning ignored the fact that the high wages
an individual businessman pays his work force will probably not
affect the demand for his own product significantly. Thus, it will
be to his advantage for other employers to pay high wages, while
not paying them himself—in other words, to espouse the high-wage
doctrine but not to practice it.

Elton Mayo's Hawthorne experiments scientifically reinforced
the argument that social responsibility might result in profit. He
argued that insufficient understanding of and concern about the
effects of modern mass production techniques could lead to dis-
ruptive and less productive behavior on the part of the worker. "But
should monotony chiefly characterize his daily work, his fears and
superstitions grow, his mental garden is uncultivated and is overrun
by the poisonous weeds of unhealthy revery. It is this attitude in
the mind-behind-the-scenes of the defeated worker which gives rise
to all forms of 'unrest.' "[47] The idea that by helping others the employer would help himself inverted the central element of the old
ideology, the "invisible hand."

The Progressive era "gave rise to an efficiency craze."[48] If any
single individual could be responsible for this craze, it was Frederick W. Taylor. In *The Principles of Scientific Management*, which
appeared in 1911, Taylor directed his arguments at American businessmen, but his influence was much wider. Lenin praised him; in
his science fiction novel *We*, Soviet author Yevgeny Zamyatin characterized Taylor as "unquestionably the greatest genius of the an-
cients,"[49] and Clemenceau advocated that scientific management be
adopted in the French arsenals and shipyards. In America, Progressive intellectuals like Croly and Brandeis were scientific management enthusiasts.

46. "Real Wages at High Peak," p. 13.
47. "The Great Stupidity," *Harper's Magazine* (July 1925), p. 231.
48. Samuel Haber, *Efficiency and Uplift* (Chicago: University of Chicago
Press, 1964), p. ix.
49. *We* (New York: Dutton, 1952), p. 33.

Taylor argued that there was "one best method" for any task, a method that could be discovered through careful, scientific study. His system attempted to "eliminate all unnecessary movements," substituting "fast for slow motions" while enforcing the standardization of methods. Taylor described his principles as a "mental revolution."[50] As such it was compatible with, even integral to, the social responsibilities of business. "Progressive employers began to recognize scientific management as a condition precedent to any substantial regularization of their employment."[51] Taylor stated that "the principal object of management should be to secure the maximum prosperity for the employer, coupled with the maximum prosperity for each employee."[52] Scientific management stood for "science, not rule of thumb; harmony, not discord; cooperation, not individualism."[53] In testimony before Congress, Taylor said: "I want to make it perfectly clear, because I do not think it is clear, that my interest, and I think the interest of every man who is in any way engaged in scientific management, must be first the welfare of the working men."[54] Whether or not scientific management actually contributed to the "welfare of the working man," it is interesting that the changes in working methods and relationships that it represented were justified in terms of the Progressive business ideology. Ida Tarbell, former muckraker, said of Taylor that "no man in the history of American industry has made a larger contribution to genuine cooperation and juster human relations."[55] Even representatives of the unions, generally distrustful of scientific management as such, became advocates of efficiency. William Green, president of the American Federation of Labor, in a paper delivered before

50. Judith K. Merkle, *Management and Ideology* (Berkeley: University of California Press, 1980), p. 2.

51. Stewart, *Unemployment Benefits*, p. 8.

52. *The Principles of Scientific Management* (1911; reprint, New York: W.W. Norton, 1967), p. 9.

53. Ibid., p. 140.

54. U.S. Commission on Industrial Relations, *Final Report and Testimony*, 64th Cong., 1st sess. (Washington, D.C.: U.S. Government Printing Office, 1916), vol. 1, p. 766.

55. "Making the Most of Men," *Bulletin of the Taylor Society* (February 1925), p. 80.

the Taylor Society, observed that "labor is understanding more and more that high wages and tolerable conditions of employment can be brought about through excellency in service, the promotion of efficiency and the elimination of waste."[56]

Another consequence of this expanded sphere of business competence and activity was an elevated image of the business institution and the role of businessmen. Poems were even written about the businessman's power.

> For him the coal is dug and burned,
> For him the wheels of the world are turned,
> That he may serve us all;
> Bringing the treasures from near and far,
> From broad plantation and gay bazaar
> Which answer his magic call
> Over the earth he holds his reign,
> Mine and factory, fleet and train,
> Packet and caravan.
> Who shall babble of Czars and Kings
> Here is the boss of the Scheme of Things
> Here is the Business Man![57]

Less lyrical comparisons of business power and responsibilities to those of nation states were common. One writer stated that "we can today rightly list the great powers and principalities of this world as the United States of America, the British Empire, France, Germany, Italy,—and United States Steel, Standard Oil, General Motors, General Electric, Swift's, United Fruit, and so on."[58] Wallace B. Donham of the Harvard Business School noted a parallel between "the position of the governing class in the earlier, simple societies and that of the business group in our present complex social organization. Positions of power must carry with them a sense of

56. "Labor's Ideals Concerning Management," *Bulletin of the Taylor Society* (December 1925), p. 358.

57. Berton Braley, "The Man of Business," *The Magazine of Business*, October 1920.

58. Whiting Williams, "Business Statesmanship: A New Force in Business," *The Magazine of Business*, April 1929, p. 460.

trusteeship."[59] Edward Filene declared: "Business is the government of this modern world. It may refuse for a while to function as such. It may refuse to accept its social responsibilities, and may continue to look to Washington or to God to do things which only social planning on the part of business management can do."[60] Businessmen freely and confidently acknowledged their power and responsibilities. They were in no doubt that the corporation was the dominant American institution, and that their direction of it was publicly beneficial.

The development of social policies in two companies, American Telephone and Telegraph and General Electric, illustrates the practical results of this change in ideology. The selection of these companies is based on a "most likely cases" approach—that is, if the perspective makes sense anywhere, it will be in regard to companies like these. Both companies had elaborate systems of welfare coverage for their employees, and their top officials subscribed to the Progressive business ideology. A recent in-house history of AT&T traces the origin of the "spirit of service" in the company to the presidencies of Theodore Vail and Walter Gifford. When Vail became president in May 1907, the "public was responding negatively" to the company.[61] According to Vail's biographer, his predecessor leaned toward the "public be damned" school.[62] Vail, by contrast, was acutely aware of the need to justify private ownership and control of the telephone industry to the public. He understood that power raised the problem of legitimacy. "We believe," he said, "that our company has a most vital interest in, and that our future success and prosperity depend upon the working out of the telephone and telegraph problem in a way that meets the approval of

59. Wallace B. Donham, "The Emerging Profession of Business," *Harvard Business Review*, 5 (July 1927), p. 405.

60. Edward A. Filene, *Successful Living in this Machine Age* (New York: Simon and Schuster, 1932), pp. 273–74.

61. *A Capsule History of the Bell System* (New York: American Telephone and Telegraph Company, 1975), p. 35.

62. Albert B. Paine, *Theodore N. Vail* (New York: Harper and Bros., 1921), p. 223.

the public as a whole." He recognized "a responsibility and accountability to the public."[63] An earlier historian noted "a change of spirit on the part of the American Telephone and Telegraph Company officials," between 1908 and 1916. They accepted "a broader, more far sighted view of the proper position of this great industry in our industrial and social system." [64]

Vail's appointment marked the beginning of various social policies at AT&T. In 1913 a pension, disability, and death benefit plan was introduced. The plan was justified in terms of providing employees with financial security and freeing them from anxiety about their own and their dependents' welfare.[65] The company covered the entire cost of the plan. Acknowledging that compensation for industrial accidents was a legal obligation in most states, AT&T claimed that its own plan went beyond the statutory requirements. AT&T regarded itself as a leader with respect to social policies and observed that "the trend of public opinion continues to support our belief that these provisions are no more than justice to the men and women who are devoting their working lives to the telephone service of this country."[66] In 1918 the company introduced an employee representation scheme to maintain a spirit of mutual cooperation and give employees a collective say in the conditions of their employment.

For much of Vail's presidency, which ended in 1919, AT&T officials were concerned about the possibility of government ownership of the telephone business. Vail believed that government regulation was appropriate: "Where there is no competition, there should be regulation."[67] However, he opposed government ownership, asserting that "no government owned telephone system in the world is giving as cheap and efficient service as the American public is getting."[68] About half of the sixty-eight pages in the company's

63. Annual Report of the Directors of American Telephone and Telegraph Company to the Stockholders (1911), pp. 33–34.

64. J. Warren Stehman, The Financial History of the American Telephone and Telegraph Company (Boston: Houghton Mifflin, 1925), p. 123.

65. Annual Report (1912), p. 18.

66. Annual Report (1917), p. 18.

67. A Capsule History of the Bell System, p. 44.

68. Annual Report (1913), p. 29.

1913 annual report were devoted to arguing against government ownership. The fact that under the Liberal government in Britain the Post Office had taken over the domestic telephone industry in 1912 served as a warning to AT&T officials. In the same year the company became the target for antitrust action. Vail responded by announcing that AT&T would sell its Western Union stock, thus forestalling such action. Nevertheless, in 1913 Congressman David J. Lewis of Maryland was actively advocating government owner-ship and receiving significant support. The postmaster general ap-pointed a committee to look into the matter, and in 1918 the Post Office Department actually took control of AT&T. It was, however, returned to private control the following year. After this interlude the threat of government ownership receded, although it did not disappear. Various congressmen continued to call for the "postali-zation" of the telephone system throughout the 1920s.[69]

The possibility of government takeover forced AT&T officials to confront the question of the legitimacy of private control. Under the leadership of Vail and his successor, Harry Thayer, the corporation sought justification by pointing to the service it provided and ac-knowledging its obligations for the well-being of its employees. The company had dropped the traditional doctrines of management that had contributed to its legitimacy problems in the first place. Ac-ceptance of regulation replaced hostility to government; the pre-rogative of private control based on private property rights, laissez-faire, and the postulates of social Darwinism were not asserted.

Walter Gifford, who took over in 1925, was a vigorous exponent of the progressive business ideology. "Coincident with the organi-zation of big business," he said, "has come the belief that extreme individualism must be tempered with a regard for social conse-quences"; the "autocratic captain of industry" has been replaced by "a type of management which recognizes its responsibility is three-fold—that in fact, if not in law, it is a trustee acting in the joint interests of owners, workers, and customers."[70] This respon-

69. Horace Coon, *American Telephone and Telegraph* (New York: Longmans, Green, 1939), p. 242.
70. "Prosperity," *Bell Telephone Quarterly,* January 1930, pp. 8–10.

sibility extended to the problem of unemployment. It also restrained the profit seeking impulse, since it would be contrary to sound policy for the management to earn speculative or large profits for distribution as 'melons' or extra dividends."[71] Pointing to the wide distribution of stock, Gifford claimed that AT&T was "a large democratic American institution, owned by 340,000 men and women." The company, he argued, was publicly owned and engaged in public service.[72]

Gifford firmly believed that voluntary action on the part of individuals and institutions was a substitute for state action in addressing social problems.

There are fundamentally only two methods of attending to those who in our society cannot and do not attend to themselves successfully without help. One is by government action supported by taxation. The other is by voluntary action of people interested enough to devote time and money to this part of American life . . . However, I believe it is as sound a principle in welfare work as it is in other activities that American government agencies should do nothing that other agencies can and will do . . . That the state performs certain welfare functions in the Scandinavian countries and Germany is not a valid argument that the state should perform these functions here, for neither the people nor the conditions are the same. We have an American method of voluntary action for meeting the welfare needs of our people that is in keeping with our social and political philosophy.[73]

This vision of an American alternative to European state welfare provision, which penetrated the thinking of public officials and the

71. "A Statement of Policy of the American Telephone and Telegraph Company," Bell Telephone Quarterly, January 1928, p. 2.

72. "Address to Educational Conference," Bell Telephone Quarterly, October 1924, pp. 218–20.

73. Addresses, Papers and Interviews, 1928–1937 (New York: American Telephone and Telegraph Company, 1937), p. 52.

actual policies of corporations, may account for the comparatively slow pace of development of the "welfare state" in America.[74]

In 1926 AT&T established an employee savings plan to supplement the employee stock purchase plan, and introduced a life insurance plan. In 1931 Gifford was appointed director of President Hoover's Organization on Unemployment Relief, which encouraged corporations to adopt "work spreading" policies. AT&T, in 1932, stated that in order "to spread available work so that the maximum number could be kept employed, more than half of the employees of the Bell telephone companies by the end of the year were working less than full time." According to the company, about forty-two thousand people who would otherwise have been laid off were still on the payroll because of this policy.[75] In 1933 the company stopped taking subscriptions for its employee stock purchase plan and suspended the employee savings plan because of depressed business conditions.

General Electric Company, established in 1892, started a pension scheme for its employees in 1915. Two years earlier Owen D. Young had joined GE as a vice president. Ida Tarbell, a convert to the Progressive business ideology, considered him a splendid example of the emerging "new type" of American industrialist who recognized social responsibilities and was responsive to social problems.[76] Young, himself a lawyer, attributed the development of a "new idea in management" to the fact that lawyers were beginning to occupy high management positions. "If there is one thing that a lawyer is taught," he said, "it is knowledge of trusteeship . . . Very soon we saw arising a notion that managers were no longer attorneys for stockholders, they were becoming trustees of an institution. Now that is a great change." The trustees, he added, must "administer wisely and fairly in the interest of all."[77] Young became chair-

74. See Furniss and Mitchell, "American Exceptionalism in Comparative Perspective."

75. *Annual Report* (1933), p. 6.

76. *Owen D. Young: A New Type of Industrial Leader* (New York: Macmillan, 1932).

77. "What is Right in Industry?" *General Electric Review*, April 1929, pp. 185–88.

man of the board of GE in 1923. Two years later, Samuel Untermyer, former counsel for the Pujo committee, described GE as a "public menace," but "for once accusations by this noted inquisitor fell on deaf ears. The newspapers remarked editorially that Mr. Young was chairman and nothing, therefore, could be radically wrong with GE."[78]

Gerard Swope, who was appointed president of GE in 1924, was also a leading spokesman for the progressive business ideology. Unlike Young, however, he considered an engineering background the best training for the new manager. (He himself was an engineer.) Swope claimed to "wholeheartedly accept the conception that industry [was] not primarily for profit but rather for service," by which he meant the production of good-quality products, gradual price reductions, and an increased spread of the benefits of industrial production. Stockholders were entitled to expect a "fair, regular, uniform return." Workers must be paid adequate wages, be provided with various income maintenance programs to remove financial worries, and receive financial assistance for housing (though the manufacturer must not become landlord) and access to investment opportunities. Swope drew up what became known as the Swope Plan at the beginning of the Great Depression. He advocated business "stabilization" policies and unemployment insurance schemes, arguing that business should act before the government did.[79]

GE established an unemployment insurance plan in 1930. Equal contributions were paid by workers and the company, and the plan was jointly administered. This added to a range of social policies introduced by the company since the establishment of the pension plan. In 1924 the company began providing financial assistance to workers who wanted to own their homes. Employee investment bonds had become available on an installment basis in 1920. In the same year a noncontributory life insurance plan was introduced. By 1925 the company paid out more than two million dollars to

78. *Review of Reviews* 76 (December 1927), p. 593.

79. "What Big Business Owes the Public," *The World's Work* 53 (March 1927), p. 556; "The Engineer's Place in Society," *The Survey* 51 (March 1, 1924); *The Swope Plan* (New York: The Business Bourse, 1931).

more than eighteen-hundred families of deceased employees.[80] In the same year the Senate directed the Federal Trade Commission to investigate the extent of GE's monopoly power. Its 1928 report found no monopoly. (GE officials showed less overt concern than their AT&T counterparts about the possibility of government intervention, possibly because GE was in a less exposed position.) The unemployment insurance plan was terminated in 1935 because of the passage of the federal Social Security Act, thus dashing Swope's hope of preempting government policies in this field.

Another way of appreciating the change in American businessmen's perception of their social and economic role is to look at the "professionalization" of business brought about by the emergence of the Progressive ideology. "Business," said Gifford, "is becoming a profession. To me it seems obvious that men with a responsible attitude toward business are rapidly replacing men whose chief incentive was great personal wealth."[81] In the 1920s numerous articles appeared in the business press on the "emerging profession of business." As early as 1914, Louis Brandeis observed that "business should be, and to some extent already is, one of the professions."[82] He cited Edward Filene as an example of a professional businessman. Brandeis was as optimistic as any businessman about business's capacity to solve social problems, declaring that "as the profession of business develops, the great industrial and social problems expressed in the present social unrest will one by one find solution."[83] Mary P. Follett, saying that "the word profession connotes for most people a foundation of science and a motive of service," claimed that "business management is every day coming more and more to rest on scientific foundations"—foundations that were being laid by Frederick Taylor and Elton Mayo.[84] In line with this endeavor to professionalize business, codes of ethics prolifer-

80. *Annual Report* (1925), p. 11.

81. "The Changing Character of Big Business," *The World's Work* 52 (June 1926), p. 168.

82. *Business—A Profession* (Boston: Small, Maynard, 1914), p. 1.

83. Ibid., p. 12.

84. "How Must Business Management Develop In Order to Possess the Essentials of a Profession?" in Metcalf, ed., *Business Management as a Profession*.

ated during the twenties. Business schools were to provide the training for this new profession. The founding of many of these schools was justified in terms of the professionalization of business.[85] It was only after World War I that business schools became widespread and business education common, when a "veritable craze for business education swept over the country." There were seven schools of business in 1900 and 183 in 1924.[86]

In commenting with approval on a speech by Owen D. Young, the *New Republic* described the nature of training a businessman should receive.

> He must move in a world of ideas, adequate to maintain professional standards based upon the conception of business as an integral part of society, with a cooperative function in the general welfare. He must regard as desirable full publicity for results and methods, the elimination of waste, the installation of better devices, the improvement of the product, the lowering of prices, and the raising of wages, whether or not such activities contribute to the utmost possible profit. He must understand the obligation of his concern to the industry of which it is a part, to the community of production and trade, to the employees, and to the life of the nation.[87]

In other words, the businessman must be familiar with the tenets of the Progressive business ideology. The development of this ideology, and the problems of corporate legitimacy that preceded it, gave impetus to the movement to professionalize business. The claim that business was a profession became part of the Progressive ideology and further encouraged this movement. By the end of the decade the Committee on Recent Economic Changes observed that the "profession of management is clearly emerging, and there is

85. "Is Business a Profession?" *The New Republic*, June 15, 1927, p. 85; A. Lawrence Lowell, "The Profession of Business," *Harvard Business Review* 1, (January 1923), p. 131.

86. L. C. Marshall, *The Collegiate School of Business* (Chicago: University of Chicago Press, 1928), p. 4.

87. "Is Business a Profession?" p. 85.

Table 8.1 A Comparison of Business Ideologies

	Nineteenth-century	Progressive
Goal of economic activity	Profit	Profit plus social responsibility
Methods of economic activity	Competition	Combination and cooperation
Components of economic activity	Individualized and commodified labor; numerous and powerless firms	Collectivized and humanized labor; few, large, powerful firms
Relation to public interest	Indirect result of economic activity	Direct result of economic activity
Social progress and economic activity	Quietist; nonintentional change; poverty and unemployment treated as conditions	Activist; intentional social change; poverty and unemployment treated as problems

visible an increasing professional spirit in business, which springs from and entails recognized social responsibilities."[88]

It is now possible to provide a summary picture of the economic system from this new ideological perspective. Table 8.1 compares the old and the new business ideologies in terms of the system's five elements. In the Progressive ideology, economic activity was oriented toward unselfish goals in addition to profit. Profit could be subordinated to these goals, coexistent with these goals, or viewed as a reward for the pursuit of these goals. The possibility of entertaining goals other than profit implied certain assumptions about the method of economic activity. For a business institution to voluntarily incur additional "social" costs, it must operate outside the competitive market. Combination and cooperation among business

88. Committee on Recent Economic Changes, p. 11.

institutions replaced competition. It was not until the early 1930s, with Joan Robinson's argument that perfect competition was a special case and not a paradigm, that economic theory caught up with economic reality.[89] In the Progressive ideology, cooperation replaced conflict between labor and capital, class harmony was advocated, and labor was viewed as possessing collective interests and empowered to bargain collectively. Business institutions were large and relatively few per industry, and the managers of these institutions had choices: they had power. The state occupied an ambiguous position. It was both a threat to business power and a possible ally. George Perkins vigorously defended the positive contributions the state could make to economic activity. Discussing the railroad industry, he claimed that "the injurious methods of twenty years ago in the railroad business were the ruthless competitive methods, and they have been virtually eliminated through Federal legislation." As a replacement for antitrust policy, Perkins advocated that businesses be placed under the control of a federal board "with power to licence corporations as were clearly working for and not against the public interest."[90]

In the Progressive business ideology, the public interest was a direct—for some, the paramount—goal of economic activity. It was the criterion by which the legitimacy of economic activity and institutions was evaluated, though businessmen themselves defined their "social responsibilities." The Progressive ideology was activist. In an industrial age, the material benefits of which lay all around, the business institution was the principal agent of problem solving. This was particularly true in America, where socialism could founder on Sombart's "reefs of roast beef and apple pie," where wages and consumption were higher than anywhere else. Reliance was placed on the "visible hand of management." Poverty and unemployment were identified as problems responsive to busi-

89. Joan Robinson, *The Economics of Imperfect Competition* (London: Macmillan, 1964), p. 307.

90. "Business and Government," p. 23.

ness action. Even the business cycle was potentially controllable. "It is perfectly possible," said Henry Ford, "to take the ill effect of seasons, if not the seasons, out of industry, and also the periodic depressions."[91] The firm, then, in Progressive business ideology, was pictured as a multipurpose, powerful, and socially responsible institution. Thus, social policy, in terms of the minimum constituents of a defensible policy choice, was advocated as falling within the *authority* of the business institution and representing an *efficient* use of resources. (The corporation was the best institution for the task, and social policies might even be profitable.) Moreover, it was *fair* in terms of transferring benefits to those "other parties" to industrial production.

It is easier to describe the contents of this ideology than to assess its diffusion. Although it is to be expected that the Progressive ideology was a general characteristic of large corporations, the period limits the ways of bringing evidence to bear. While an examination of both small and big businessmen's views would be preferable, big businessmen are more likely to have had their views and attitudes reported in the business press. Thus, the focus is only on the views of officials of large corporations. Using Berle and Means's list of the largest nonfinancial corporations in 1929, I have selected the top seventy-five firms and identified the chairmen and/ or president, yielding a total of 106 businessmen. I searched the *Reader's Guide to Periodical Literature* (1920–30) for statements, interviews, and articles by or about these businessmen. This material was then analyzed in terms of ideological content.[92] The writings or interviews of 28 percent of these businessmen concerned ideological themes—a large enough proportion to analyze, though our findings must be tentative. These thirty businessmen (see table 8.2) represented all three sectors—railways, utilities, and manufacturing companies—in the Berle and Means study. A further twenty who appeared in the periodical literature in this period did not

91. *My Life and Work*, p. 133.
92. See Maynard S. Seider, "American Big Business Ideology: A Content Analysis of Executive Speeches," *American Sociological Review* 39 (December 1974).

Table 8.2   Business Ideologies in the Top 75 U.S. Firms, 1929

	Nineteenth-century	Progressive	Uncertain
Managers	17% ($N = 24$)	79%	4%
Owners	0% ($N = 6$)	100%	0%

discuss or reveal ideological positions. Of the thirty, sixteen can be classified as holding the Progressive ideology, and nine more as probably progressive. What is remarkable is that only two businessmen can be classified as holding the nineteenth-century ideology—Newcomb Carlton of Western Union and the younger J. P. Morgan. Two more can be classified as probables, and one case is inconclusive.

As the Berle and Means study was used, it is possible to return to the question of the motivational significance of the separation of ownership from control. Managerialist theory suggests that officials of management-controlled corporations would be more likely to hold the Progressive ideology. Most of the Progressive idealogues were indeed officials from management-controlled corporations, but the preponderance of such corporations in the analysis makes it difficult to draw firm conclusions. Twenty-four officials of management-controlled firms are among the thirty who can be identified in terms of ideology; of these, nineteen were Progressive or probably Progressive. Interestingly, all four exponents of nineteenth-century ideology were also officials of management-controlled corporations. The six officials of owner-controlled corporations all held the Progressive ideology. Neither were management-controlled corporations officials any more likely to commit themselves publicly to an ideological position. Some 72 percent of the management-controlled corporation officials and 70 percent of the owner-controlled corporation officials did not discuss or reveal an ideological position. It would therefore appear that the 1920s saw the ascendancy of the Progressive ideology among large corporations, irrespective of control type.

The contents of this ideology would strike a familiar chord

among today's corporate officials. In fact, the Progressive ideology is an early version of the postwar "managerial" ideology or the "new" ideology that Robert Heilbroner analyzed in the 1960s.[93] Heilbroner cites five major constituents of the new ideology: the distinction between modern and old-fashioned capitalism, professional responsibility, the need for large-scale organization, stress on human values, and a new legitimacy for the roles of labor and government. As we have seen, these themes were actually the discovery of the corporate official of the 1920s, and the ideology that they constitute is an enduring characteristic of twentieth-century corporate capitalism.

It is appropriate to finish this chapter by evaluating the effectiveness of social responsibility as a solution to the problem of corporate legitimacy. The 1920s saw the spread of the progressive ideology and corporate social policies and, for the first time, general social and political accommodation to corporate capitalism as the dominant economic form. To conclude that the corporation achieved legitimacy in the 1920s does not mean that this was an achievement of ideological and policy change, but it is a plausible connection to make. The decline of the corporation as a political issue in party platforms and as a target for antitrust policy (see chapter 7) corresponds with the ideological change and the development of social policy. "Once upon a time Big Business was in bad odor. That was in the Roosevelt era—including the first term of Woodrow Wilson . . . Now all that has changed."[94] Press accounts such as this one in the 1920s also testify to the new legitimacy of corporations. These accounts linked ideological change to the change in popular attitudes. "Here is a new conception of business which explains in large part the changed attitude of public opinion and government toward it."[95] The favorable disposition of government was symbolized by what happened to the Federal Trade Commission in the

93. "The View from the Top: Reflections on a Changing Business Ideology," in Earl F. Cheit, ed., *The Business Establishment* (New York: Wiley, 1964).
94. *Outlook* 151 (March 27, 1929), p. 492.
95. *Literary Digest* 86 (December 5, 1925), p. 5.

1920s: "Where the FTC had been set up to discourage monopoly it now espoused the cause of the self-regulation of business."[96]

The Progressive ideology captured the minds of public officials as well as big businessmen. Government willingly deferred to business. Comparing Coolidge unfavorably with Roosevelt and Wilson, a New Republic article said that "what we are now witnessing is a conscientious and thoroughgoing withdrawal of political government from the field of public policy ... carried out by a chief executive who is more genuinely a delegate of the business and financial estate than any President for a generation." This withdrawal met with popular approval; a majority of the electorate were more favorably disposed to "control by private interests" than ever before.[97] Yet it was the election of Herbert Hoover that signalled the triumph of the Progressive business ideology and the perception of the corporation as a highly functional social, as well as economic, institution. Since his time as secretary of commerce under Harding, Hoover had been an open supporter of corporate social responsibility. He "considered it part of the duties of the Secretary of Commerce to help bring business to a realization of its responsibilities and to suggest methods of its own cures."[98]

The notion of business social responsibility dominated American social reform efforts in the 1920s. The President's Conference on Unemployment in 1921 recommended business stabilization practices. Senate hearings on unemployment became forums for businessmen to describe their solutions and to denounce public-sector involvement by pointing to European developments. Hoover retained his faith in the private sector even as late as 1931. "We have had one proposal after another which amounts to a dole from

96. Schlesinger, The Crisis of the Old Order (Boston: Houghton Mifflin, 1957), p. 65. James Weinstein, in his fine discussion of the period 1900–18, also finds businessmen effective in managing public authorities. However, his work focuses on the role of the National Civic Federation and individual businessmen rather than specifically on business ideology and corporate social policies, other than workman's compensation. James Weinstein, The Corporate Ideal in the Liberal State (Boston: Beacon Press, 1968).

97. "Government Abdicates," The New Republic, May 20, 1925, p. 333.

98. The Memoirs of Herbert Hoover, vol. 2 (New York: Macmillan, 1952), p. 167.

the Federal Treasury. The largest is that of unemployment insurance. I have long advocated such insurance as an additional measure of safety against rainy days, but only through private enterprise or through the cooperation of industry and labor itself."[99] Again, the belief among public officials that business held the solution to social problems explains the American public sector's reluctance to get involved in social policies. A final indication of the new legitimacy of large corporations in the 1920s is provided by the upswing in merger activity. The number of mergers increased from 89 in 1919 to 221 in 1928.[100]

We have seen that the development of corporate social responsibility was accompanied by the growing legitimacy of corporations. That the new ideology penetrated the thinking of public officials is demonstrated by their acceptance of the corporation as the major institution to address social problems. This suggests that social responsibility was the central factor in the public acceptance of corporate power in the 1920s. It was not, however, the only factor involved: the legitimacy of corporations was assisted by the decline of the Socialist party. This decline may be linked to the influence of the new ideology, yet it was also the result of the difficult situation the party encountered when the United States entered World War I. Divisions over the party's antiwar stance, the government's repressive reaction, and Eugene Debs's illness muted the most radical criticism of corporate power. One might also take the position that the economic situation was generally propitious for the acceptance of corporate power. But while the 1920s is usually considered a prosperous decade, a severe depression occurred in 1921, and smaller ones in 1924 and 1927, and for much of the decade unemployment was over 10 percent. Even if one accepts that the decade saw rising prosperity, there is no simple relationship between this trend and corporate legitimacy. As an illustration, the 1960s represent the longest sustained period of economic growth since at least the 1920s, yet these years saw a great decline in public confidence in business—a point to which we will return in the next chapter.

99. Commons, *History of Labor*, vol. 3, p. 159.
100. Committee on Recent Economic Changes, p. 221.

John Kenneth Galbraith has said that the oldest of economic problems is "that of the mitigation or regulation of economic power."[101] He describes three solutions to this problem. One is competition in the market, and the second is control by the state. (The third is Galbraith's own theory of countervailing power, though the weakness of American unions makes it difficult to take this seriously.) While state control is not a solution businessmen normally would choose, competition in the market appeared to have broken down by the turn of the century. Businessmen's approach to the problem was neither to deny their power nor to yield to the state. Instead, they attempted to persuade those affected by this power that they were using it appropriately. The language of persuasion was the Progressive business ideology.

101. "Countervailing Power," *American Economic Review* 44 (May 1954), p. 1.

nine

Plus ça change: From the 1920s to the 1980s

Two nonexclusive paths lead to the maintenance of power: coercion and persuasion. Following the first, a nonstate political institution may find itself in conflict with the state. The use of coercion dramatizes an institution's power and challenges the state's putative monopoly of the means of violence. Other institutions and groups in society are likely to demand that the state take action to protect its monopoly. The consequence is a threat to the power the institution desired to maintain. For the corporate prince it is, then, better to be loved than feared. States themselves, even those which have the most complete monopoly on coercion, avoid exclusive dependence upon it; hence the importance of ideology in a concept like totalitarianism.

The second path is less risky. Persuasion that the institution does not possess power (which is the message of classical business ideology and, for that matter, pluralism) or that the exercise of power is legitimate (which is the message of the Progressive business ideology) makes coercion unnecessary. Crises of legitimacy occur when persuasion breaks down. This breakdown initiates a search for new grounds of persuasion. Following the second path, American corporate officials moved from a denial of power to a denial of selfishness. The Progressive business ideology and its social policy consequences provided a basis for building a new consensus on the legitimacy of corporate power.

Sixty years since this consensus was constructed, corporate social responsibility remains businessmen's preferred response to threats to corporate power, and they continue to present it in vigorous terms, as if it were a recent discovery. In the 1960s and 1970s, American corporations encountered the most severe questioning of their power since the Progressive era. Seymour Martin Lipset and William Schneider write that the "period from 1965 to 1975 . . . was one of enormous growth in anti-business sentiment." In 1973 a majority of Americans supported the proposition that "for the good of the country, many of our largest companies ought to be broken up into smaller companies."[1] The jacket of another study proclaims: "Seldom have businessmen been more shaken than by the combination of anti-business public sentiment and the revelation of political and corporate scandals that marked the late sixties and the mid-seventies."[2] From 1966 to 1981, "confidence in the leaders of major companies fell farther and faster than confidence in the leaders of any other major institution."[3]

Analysis suggests that the problem for American businessmen is "a generalized feeling that business puts profits ahead of human concerns and that it lacks compassion and social responsibility."[4] So contemporary businessmen, apparently unaware that they echo an earlier generation of corporate officials, assert their heightened sensitivity to social concerns. The Committee for Economic Development, an organizational counterpart to the National Civic Federation, observed in the early 1970s that "significant" changes were "under way in the corporate institution and managerial outlook," and described "the modern professional manager" as "a trustee balancing the interests of many diverse participants and constituents."[5] Meanwhile, a commentator warns that the "less voluntary social action U.S. companies take, the more it will be imposed by

1. *The Confidence Gap: Business, Labor, and Government in the Public Mind* (New York: Free Press, 1983), p. 31.

2. Leonard Silk and David Vogel, *Ethics and Profits* (New York: Simon and Schuster, 1976).

3. *The Confidence Gap*, p. 358.

4. Ibid., p. 359.

5. Committee for Economic Development, *Social Responsibility of Business Corporations* (New York, 1971), p. 22.

big government."[6] And a president was elected who, Hoover-like, looked to the private sector as a real alternative to state involvement in addressing social problems, while his attorney general declared that "bigness in business is not necessarily bad" and merger activity increased.[7] The parallels extend to the questioning and criticism of corporate power, to which corporate social responsibility may still hold a satisfactory answer. Ralph Nader, most feared of corporate critics, is a modern muckraker. Critics target the use of power—the quality and safety of products, for example—rather than the possession of power. There is still no socialism in the United States.

Some things have changed since the 1920s. With the 1935 Social Security Act and the development of public-sector income maintenance policies, corporate social policies shifted emphasis and turned in new directions, in line with wider social movements. As a result, many corporations now recognize specific obligations to minorities, and the art world has become a prime beneficiary of corporate philanthropy. Another piece of legislation in 1935, the Internal Revenue Act, also affected corporate social responsibility. By making corporate gifts of up to 5 percent of income tax deductible, the state began financially contributing to the process of corporate legitimization. Other than the members of the Minneapolis "5 percent club," corporations generally do not come close to the statutory limit. The legality of corporate philanthropy was decided in the 1950s, when a stockholder's claim against a New Jersey manufacturing company that gave money to Princeton University was denied.

Corporate social responsibility is an enduring characteristic of large American corporations, an outcome of their search for legitimacy and evidence of their political nature. It is underdeveloped in most European corporations, because in Europe the state is traditionally viewed as the source of social policy. In addition, the corporate sector developed less vigorously and criticism of corpo-

6. David F. Linowes, *The Corporate Conscience* (New York: Hawthorn, 1974), p. 9.
7. William French Smith quoted in the *Economist*, October 31, 1981, p. 20.

rate power in Europe is more likely to be socialist, not caring to distinguish between "good" and "bad" corporations. The more profound the criticism of the corporation, the less likely it is that the progressive business ideology and social policy will be thought effective in addressing legitimacy problems. It is estimated that the average British company contributes less than 0.5 percent of pretax profits, in contrast to the 2 percent of pretax profits contributed by American companies—and the British are generous by continental standards.[8] Of course, these are average figures and there is considerable variation among companies. But the point is that while any social spending by a "business" institution is surprising, corporate social policies are necessarily limited by economic constraints and are grounded in legitimacy problems, not social problems as such. So, despite all the publicity given to corporate social responsibility by presidential exhortations and corporate officials themselves, promise will always exceed performance.

What support does contemporary corporate activity provide for this explanation of corporate social responsibility? To answer this question, the following hypotheses must be evaluated:

1. Corporate social policy is associated with large firms, irrespective of control type.
2. Corporate social policy depends on a minimum level of profit, but its amount is not associated with increases in profit.
3. Corporate social policy increases as public hostility to corporations and the likelihood of government intervention increases.
4. Corporate social policy is associated with firms whose decision makers operate within the framework of the progressive business ideology.

The first hypothesis takes the size of the firm as an indication of market power and of the visibility of that power. As the firm becomes more powerful, more conspicuous, and more likely to encounter legitimacy problems, it will be more likely to make social

8. *The Financial Times*, May 4, 1988, p. 22.

policy. Control type—management or ownership—is not expected
to influence social policy; whoever is in control of a large firm will
encounter the problems that power entails. One might expect that
owner-controllers are more likely to advance the private property
justification in response to legitimacy problems. Yet the evidence
presented earlier does not support this expectation, perhaps because owner-controllers have only a minority control position and
because the firms and the populations they affect are so large that
the privateness of property is difficult to assert.

A threshold of profit is a requirement for corporate social policies. But more profit will not necessarily produce more social policies and greater corporate generosity. It is power rather than profit
that needs legitimacy. Although legitimacy is sought through the
denial of the selfish pursuit of profit, a stronger association with
size than profit is expected for corporate social policy. Social policy
will increase as the size of the firm rather than its profit increases.

When public hostility to business rises, and the likelihood of
interference with corporate power increases, then so will social
policy effort. As the third hypothesis suggests, it is the perception
of how power is exercised as well as its possession that generates
legitimacy problems. The fourth hypothesis appears tautological,
and in a sense it is, for the Progressive business ideology implies
corporate social policy. The ideology achieves full meaning only
when it is accompanied by this activity; otherwise it is "empty
rhetoric."[9]

However, because a set of ideas "logically" entails certain actions
does not mean that those actions will necessarily follow; other constraints may be sufficiently severe to prohibit the actions. This
means that the relationship between ideas and actions is worth
empirical investigation, as analysts of public-sector social policies
know. They have, for example, hypothesized a relationship between
social democratic ideology and the level of public social policy efforts. On the other hand, convergence theory—the view that the
process of industrialization forces growing social similarity, cross-
culturally and regardless of ideology—stresses constraints on actors

9. See MacIntyre, "A Mistake About Causality in Social Science."

that are sufficiently severe to make their beliefs irrelevant to the course of social change. To focus on specifically political constraints, the need to win elections or bureaucratic inertia can force leaders of political parties to deviate from principles and platforms. Evidence with which to assess these four hypotheses is drawn from a comparison of the social policy efforts of *Fortune* 500 companies. The Council for Advancement and Support of Education lists more than nine hundred corporations that participate in its matching gift programs; collectively, they gave $48 million through these programs in 1981. These lists provide a means of categorizing individual companies according to the level of participation they agreed to.[10] As firm-by-firm identification is possible, it is a more useful indicator of social policy than the aggregate data of corporate income tax returns. However, it is not exhaustive, since some social policy makers do not participate in the matching-gift programs.

Of the 1983 *Fortune* 500 Industrials, 290 participated in varying degrees in the matching-gift programs. Companies could choose to give to education, to health and welfare institutions, to cultural organizations, or to any combination of these. Education was much the most popular, followed by cultural organizations, and then health and welfare institutions. Companies could also choose to match, double, triple, or quadruple employee gifts. From this information one can distinguish broad categories (low, medium, and high) that reflect different levels of commitment to corporate giving. These categories do not reflect money that was actually spent; that depends on the number of employees in the company who were willing to contribute. The list of 1983 *Fortune* 500 Industrials, which provides data from 1982, was used on the assumption that decisions about social policies in 1983 would be made on the basis of the companies' circumstances in the previous year.

In line with *Fortune*'s ranking system, firm size is measured in sales rather than assets. As anticipated, a clear association emerged between the variables of size and social policy. Among the top 100

10. Council for Advancement and Support of Education, "Double Your Dollar, 1983–1984" (Washington, D.C., 1983).

companies, 82 had some level of social policy commitment. This figure then drops steadily across the size categories to a low of 26 companies engaging in social policy among the 401–500. Table 9.1 shows that size also affects the level of social policy. For example, 14 of the top 100 companies were in the high social policy category (37 percent of all companies in this category), whereas only 3 of the bottom 100 achieved this level. Unfortunately, the data say nothing about the effect of control type on social policy.

Profit is defined as net income as a percentage of equity, a standardized measure given in the *Fortune* 500 listings. As expected, only the absence of a profit has any impact on social policy level: almost half of the loss-makers in 1982 made no social policy. The low (0–9 percent), medium (10–15 percent), and high (16 percent and above) categories of profit have little effect on social policy. It is true that a slightly higher percentage of companies in the high profit category are in the high social policy category, but this is probably linked to the effect of firm size. Nine of these 14 firms are in *Fortune*'s top 100. In fact, at the other end of the social policy scale, a slightly higher percentage of the high profit group than the low or medium group make no social policy. Simply because it is easier for a company to finance social policy does not mean it will commit itself to more social policy. Table 9.1 provides some support for the view that once a company has crossed the threshold from loss to profit, its social policy commitment does not automatically increase with profit[11]; and it provides strong support for the claim that social policy as a legitimation device is linked to power (size), not profit. The statistical significance of this link is indicated in the large chi-square for size and social policy, in contrast to the small chi-square for profit and social policy. The gammas suggest a moderately strong association (-0.48) between size and social policy, and almost no association (0.04) between profit and social policy. The negative sign is a result of using the *Fortune* categories

11. Katherine M. McElroy and John J. Siegfried do find a relationship between profit and corporate giving, though giving increases less than proportionately to an increase in profit. See "The Effect of Firm Size and Mergers on Corporate Philanthropy," in Betty Bock et al., eds., *The Impact of Modern Corporation* (New York: Columbia University Press, 1984), p. 22.

Table 9.1 Social Policy Commitment of 1983 *Fortune* 500
Companies

	FIRM RANK				
Social Policy	1–100	101–200	201–300	301–400	401–500
None	18%	24%	36%	58%	74%
Low	47%	40%	44%	32%	20%
Medium	21%	27%	14%	4%	3%
High	14%	9%	6%	6%	3%
	100%	100%	100%	100%	100%
	(N=100)	(N=100)	(N=100)	(N=100)	(N=100)

Chi-square = 106.5 with 12df. significant at the 0.001 level
Gamma = −0.48

	PROFIT*			
	Loss	Low	Medium	High
None	48%	38%	39%	43%
Low	33%	42%	39%	33%
Medium	17%	12%	15%	14%
High	2%	8%	8%	11%
	100%	100%	101%	101%
	(N=58)	(N=146)	(N=155)	(N=132)

Chi-square = 8.3 with 9df. not significant
Gamma = 0.04

	INDUSTRY	
	Oil, Chemical, Tobacco	Other
None	26%	45%
Low	42%	36%
Medium	17%	13%
High	15%	6%
	100%	100%
	(N=84)	(N=416)

Chi-square = 15.6 with 3df. significant at the 0.002 level
Gamma = −0.33

Note: Percentages may not total 100 due to rounding error.
*Profit data on nine firms missing.

where 1–100 are the largest firms and 401–500 are the smallest, such that a high social policy score is likely to be accompanied by a "low" (1–100) size score. For nine of the Fortune 500 no comparable information on profit was available and none of them made social policy, but they were not included in the analysis.

The third hypothesis is more difficult to examine. It is possible, however, to distinguish industries in terms of their popularity. It is expected that firms in the least popular industries will make more social policy. In the early 1980s the oil, chemical, and tobacco industries, of all the industries represented in the Fortune 500, had the lowest favorability ratings.[12] Sorting out these industries in terms of their social policy commitment provides some information with which to assess the third hypothesis. Table 9.1 shows that firms in these least popular industries are more likely to make social policy. Of these firms, 74 percent make social policies, compared to 55 percent of firms in all the other industries. For all the levels of social policy commitment the percentages are in the direction predicted. The chi-square indicates that the relationship between unpopular industries and social policy is statistically significant, and the gamma (-0.33) suggests a low-to-moderate association.

When size is taken into account, the association between unpopular industries and social policy still holds. Some 90 percent of the firms in unpopular industries in the top-100 category make social policy, as opposed to 78 percent of the others. For the other four size groups the figures are 83 percent and 74 percent, 71 percent and 63 percent, 44 percent and 42 percent, and 40 percent and 25 percent, respectively. And 34 percent of the most generous firms are oil, chemical, or tobacco companies, although companies from these industries constitute only 17 percent of all firms. Nor are they more likely to make social policy because they have higher profits: the unpopular firms in all profit categories are more likely to make social policy. Incidentally, while the oil, chemical, and tobacco industries fare worst in public opinion, this is not because these are

12. Opinion Research Corporation communication with author; and Lipset and Schneider, The Confidence Gap, p. 196–97.

the industries with highest profits. The industry medians provided by *Fortune* place at least the oil and chemical industries out of the top flight of profit-makers. (No information is given on the tobacco industry.) However, these industries may be perceived as high profit-makers by the public, and this perception may account in part for their unpopularity.

Little can be said here about the fourth hypothesis, because information on the ideology of corporate officials requires survey research that is not available. The earlier data from the 1920s suggests a link between Progressive ideology and social policy. Twenty-two of Berle and Means's top seventy-five companies had officials who held the Progressive ideology, and eighteen of these companies were also identified as making social policy.

A more comprehensive and precise social policy measure, time-series analysis, and additional information on ideology and control type will increase confidence in these conclusions about the conditions that give rise to corporate social policy. We may also wish to incorporate additional political hypotheses about, for example, the effect that the rising expectations of recipients have on corporate social policy effort. The Opinion Research Corporation has repeatedly found that two-thirds of the public agree with the statement "Business has an obligation to help society, even if it means making less profit."[13] Or we may wish to distinguish between attitudes to corporate power among the masses and the elite, and how this affects the targeting of corporate social policies. A corporation's target groups for social policy are unlikely to be the same as a government's. Institutional legitimacy, in the case of the corporation, would recommend some recipients over others—for example, museums instead of mothers with dependent children. With corporate giving, elites are as likely to become charity cases as the poor. Nor will corporations wish their gifts to excite controversy.

Further, corporations that make the most social policies are likely to be the ones that contribute most to such traditionally recognized forms of business political activity as campaign contributions. Business interest group and electoral activity—the traditional

---

13. Lipset and Schneider, *The Confidence Gap*, p. 175.

focus of political scientists—is not, in money terms, as significant a corporate activity as social responsibility. Corporate political action committees raised $127 million in 1984 compared to $3 billion spent on social programs the previous year.[14] Corporations that form political action committees are likely to be large, powerful, and concerned about threats to their power or anxious to extend their power. A recent study confirms that firm size, regulation, and market concentration all are related to the formation of these committees. Additional support comes from an investigation of corporate political activities in Britain, where firm size and state involvement in the industry are most clearly related to the formation of corporate government relations divisions.[15] As it is, this analysis of the *Fortune* 500 gives preliminary support to the claim that the theory of the corporation as a political institution, derived from a study of early corporate America, continues to be relevant to contemporary corporate activity.

This depiction of historical continuity is at odds with a recent sociological analysis of business corporations. Michael Useem, in *The Inner Circle*, identifies three "eras" of capitalism: family (nineteenth century), managerial (twentieth century pre-1950), and institutional (post-1950, particularly since the 1970s). Useem argues that social responsibility and the Progressive ideology are particular attributes of institutional capitalism. The historical evidence, however, suggests a different evolution than the one Useem describes, or at least a different chronology. Social responsibility predates "institutional capitalism." Useem defines the institutional era in terms of the number of interlocking directorships. Either he is mistaken about the required number of these directorships, or they are neither a necessary nor sufficient condition for social responsibility. (The Pujo Committee revealed J. P. Morgan's directorships in thirty-nine companies in 1913.)

14. Barbara Bardes, Mack C. Shelley II, and Steffen W. Schmidt, *American Government and Politics Today: The Essentials* (St. Paul: West, 1986), p. 264.

15. Gary J. Andres, "Business Involvement in Campaign Finance: Factors Influencing the Decision to Form a Corporate PAC," PS 18 (Spring 1985), p. 218; and Wyn Grant, *Business and Politics in Britain* (London: Macmillan, 1987), pp. 96–99.

The imaginative thesis of an "inner circle" finds room for outside threats to business power, but the analytical focus is the internal social organization of business. While Useem's analysis does recognize the unbusinesslike or noneconomic nature of corporate social activities, the more his account focuses on organizations at the expense of external threats the less we understand why they took this form. His account of organizational and bureaucratic processes does not fill in the connections to specific corporate attitudes and activities. Useem writes that the "intercorporate management network . . . is the engine behind the rise of the class wide principles associated with institutional capitalism."[16] However, corporate togetherness might as easily reinforce greedy impulses as foster charitable ones. Interlocking directorates facilitate communication and thus enhance business centralization and power. Insofar as they indicate business power, they will be associated with social responsibility. For social responsibility and the Progressive ideology originated as a response to threats to business power. They were fashioned in the conflict and interaction of businessmen, intellectuals, and politicians at the beginning of this century, not towards the end.

This book is about how corporations in twentieth-century America have defended their power. So long as the critics of corporate power are willing to distinguish between good and bad corporations—that is, to allow their criticism to fall into categories sired in an association between corporate and public officials at the turn of the century—then the Progressive business ideology and corporate social policy will be an adequate defense. The far frontier of criticism in America was established during the Progressive era. To push back this frontier, and to anticipate the breakdown of the Progressive ideology of social responsibility, is to pose the question of whether the necessarily limited benevolence of corporations makes private control of them tolerable. Having ruled out perfectly competitive capitalism as utopian, we finally arrive at the position from which political scientists usually begin analyses of corporations:

16. *The Inner Circle: Large Corporations and the Rise of Business Political Activity in the U.S. and U.K.* (New York: Oxford University Press, 1984), p. 178.

democratic theory. Dictatorship, however benevolent, is no longer acceptable in government. If democracy makes the exercise of power by government legitimate, how is the exercise of corporate power different? We have seen that even corporate officials are no longer satisfied to rely on the private property justification. Do corporate officials, unlike government officials, need the prospect of the huge incentives that private control provides in order to make good decisions? Do the benefits of these incentives compensate for the misallocation of resources that are expected to accompany private control in imperfect or monopolistic conditions? Do corporate decisions require more expertise than government decisions, thus precluding democratic control? If the answer is yes, is expertise in money-making the right sort of expertise?

These are not new questions, but neither are they familiar. While the current vogue for privatization suggests that corporate power is in no immediate danger, officials must provide a defense of private ownership, perhaps by claiming that the unexciting experiences with nationalization or command economies abroad exhaust the alternatives, or pointing to the historical (if not logical) link between private ownership in business and the development of democratic control in government.[17] If such arguments fail, they, like the first generation of corporate officials, will need to seek new grounds for legitimacy. It is difficult to imagine these new grounds without a significant surrender of corporate power to some form of democratic control for the first time in America.

17. For an insightful discussion of the relationship between capitalism and democracy, see Robert Dahl, *Dilemmas of Pluralist Democracy* (New Haven: Yale University Press, 1982).

Index